D1370677

From the Books of

Barbara L. Chestnut

Techniques of CLASSIC Color Photography

gift from my brother
Christmas 1981

Techniques of CLASSIC Color Photography

Text by David Gibbon

Designed and Produced by Ted Smart

CHARTWELL
BOOKS, INC.

We live in a colorful world. Not only strong, vibrant colors, although there are plenty of these to be seen, but also soft, subtle and gentle colors. Without light there are no colors and, indeed, color changes in hue and intensity according to the level and angle of the light reflected from it. Photography, too, depends on light. A lens gathers and focuses light; a shutter allows a measured amount of light to pass – to a film which consists of a light-sensitive emulsion that, when processed, renders permanent the image we wish to capture.

The photographic image – particularly in color – nowadays plays an important, accepted and established part in all our lives. We rely on it, whether in the form of cinematic or television film or still pictures, to provide us with information about places, people and events. We also rely on it, together with the printed or spoken word, to educate or inform us about subjects which, otherwise, we would have no way of seeing for ourselves. We can 'freeze' action and analyze it split second by split second, studying each small movement to better understand its effect; we can send cameras to the bottom of the oceans to record life at seemingly impossible depths, and we can send them out to the edges of the solar system; we can show things that only the microscope can see, and we can make all this visual information available to millions of people all over the world. We now accept, and take for granted, all the photographic information with which we are surrounded every day, but, in addition to its primary function of supplying information, photography can appeal straight to the emotions, in much the same way as can painting, sculpture or music. We can be moved – emotionally affected – by the content or subject matter of a photograph, or – and this is what should interest us – by the way the photographer has seen and interpreted it. To a considerable extent, of course, photography is directed, particularly for such purposes as advertising and fashion. Nevertheless, individual photographers still bring to such subjects their own style or interpretation; they may even become well known for it and influence the whole area of photography in which they are involved. But it is when photographers take pictures for themselves or are asked to work within very broad limits that we start to see, to a greater or lesser extent, interpretive involvement. If we were to ask three different, competent and involved photographers to present their interpretation of almost any subject we should probably find that they would produce three quite different sets of pictures; the same subject seen from three different emotional, and visual, angles. Of course, the same thing would happen if we were to ask three painters to carry out the same task and it is the similarities between the two mediums that has led, ever since the beginnings of photography, to controversy regarding its acceptance as an art form. 'Painting is art – photography is not' has long been the widely accepted view, and it may well be so, but it surely matters very little. There are good and bad painters just as there are good and bad photographers, and who is to say which is which? It depends very much on timing; yesterday's masterpiece can become today's cliché and a hitherto disregarded work can suddenly be attributed to a master and achieve immediate fame. This already happens with painting and, to a lesser extent because of the comparative newness of the medium, is happening with photography.

Pretentiousness exists in photography of course, but, again because of its relatively short history, not to the same extent as in some other art forms. It is very seldom that a photograph provokes a query as to the name of the photographer. We are far more likely to ask questions as to its content, such as 'who is it?' 'where was it taken?' or, maybe, 'what does it say, or mean, to me?' Perhaps this is one of the strengths of photography; the photograph has to stand on its own to a very large extent and no-one has any reason to be in awe of it. We may be interested, at some stage, to know the photographer's identity or we may not; we are familiar enough with photographs to be able to reject what we don't like and accept what we do on the basis of our own judgement and nothing else. Any 'art' there is in photography surely lies in seeing or visualizing the picture to begin with; without that there can be no good pictures. Translating the original idea into a finished product can be put down to craft or expertise, both of which can be taught.

The term 'commercial photography' immediately suggests photography taken for a specific purpose, be it to advertise a product, appear on a package, adorn a calendar or magazine, or whatever. While this is, of course, true for the bulk of the photography used in, particularly, advertising, it is also true to say that a considerable amount of photography that is used for a variety of purposes is obtained from stock sources. This was not always so, however, simply because there were no stocks of pictures to call on in the early days. A few specialized agencies were gradually set up over the years to syndicate, primarily, news and features, but, these apart, if photography was required it had to be commissioned. With the advent of color films, allied to more sophisticated methods of reproduction, the demand for color photography increased, not only in quantity but also in diversity of subject matter. How far we have traveled along this road may be judged from the enormous variety, in style and content, of the photographs in this present volume; all drawn from the files of one such stock photographic source – Colour Library International.

A fair question to ask is: 'When does a photograph become a commercial photograph?' It may be supposed that as soon as a photograph is sold for a particular product, be it a calendar, a book, an advertisement, a travel brochure, or in one of the many other ways in which we see color pictures employed, then it becomes a commercial photograph. On the other hand, it could be argued that commercial photography is only that which is specifically commissioned for a stated purpose.

As has already been mentioned, all the photographs in this book are from one company, so it may be worth considering, for a few moments, stock color libraries, or agencies, and how they work. To begin with, there is certainly no doubt that such enterprises are commercial; their livelihood depends on selling copyright – the least possible for the greatest return – to people who wish to use the pictures they hold. A percentage of the fee they charge is then passed on to the particular photographer concerned and, depending on how good the libraries or agencies are at their job, more and more photographers approach them for representation. In this way they gradually build up a considerable stock of pictures, either specializing in a particular field they feel they know best and which will produce the best results, or looking for the widest possible range of subject matter they wish to handle, so that they can approach and satisfy an increasing number of different clients. Most of these agencies rely on the photographers they represent to send them regular submissions of work but they exercise, in most cases, no more than an advisory control over the subjects the photographers wish to shoot. They can inform a particular photographer that a client is looking for a certain type of picture, shot in that photographer's style, but they are, after all, dealing with freelance photographers who may not be free, at that moment, to drop everything they are doing for the by no means guaranteed possibility of a sale. The company represented in this book, however, works in quite a different way. A selected number of freelance photographers are, indeed, represented, and these have been, over the years, added to as, inevitably, others fall away for one reason or another, but the essential difference lies in the fact that the bulk of the work in their files has been taken by photographers who are employed by them full time, or who are employed by them for an agreed period of time to undertake a specific commission for them. In this way, the majority of the work is directed by the company without, necessarily, any particular client in mind, and the resulting pictures are all owned by the company, to do with as they wish. As anyone who has been involved in such things these days will know, financing all the photographic trips, booking models, hotels, travel etc., can result in quite horrifying expenditure, and it could be argued that this is a more costly way of acquiring photographs than accepting them from freelance sources. This may possibly be true, but it is the price that is paid for control, and control is a very valuable commodity in photography. Lest it should be thought that control means stereotyped photography, then the pictures in the book will have to provide the answer, and the viewer will have to make up his or her mind on this. It must be said that the pictures are representative in that there is about the same proportion of freelance, commissioned and employed photographers' work in the book as is held in the company's files.

'Control' in the sense that it is used here does not mean curbing any individuality that a photographer may bring to his work. It simply means that a photographer can be sent wherever he is needed, be it into the studio or to South America, to take pictures that are required for a special project or because they would provide a useful addition to the files. From then on, however, although the photographer is provided with a brief, it is up to him how he interprets what he sees in front of him; after all, this is what he brings to the job; anyone can be taught, in a relatively short time, how to handle the controls of a camera and, while an ability to 'see' the telling picture can be developed and encouraged, something has to be there to start with; it is this that separates the technician from the 'creative' photographer.

While it is obviously true to say that a 'bad' camera – i.e. one in which the lens gives poor definition and the shutter inaccurate exposure times – will deliver poor pictures, it is as incorrect to say that a 'good' camera will always produce good pictures as it is to say that a 'good' piano will always play good music. Both of them depend on the operator, performer, artist – call him what you will. It has been said so many times that it hardly bears repeating, but *it is the man behind the camera who makes the picture; the camera only does his bidding.* It never ceases to amaze; the assumption that the possession of an expensive, sophisticated camera should almost guarantee good pictures and the disappointment when it is discovered that the camera has accurately recorded and exposed on film just what it has been pointed at and focused on – no more and no less!

As photographers, we have at our disposal a wealth of highly sophisticated equipment with which we can alter the 'straightforward' appearance of our subjects. We can use telephoto lenses or wide-angle lenses to alter the apparent perspective and introduce all sorts of distortions; we can throw backgrounds and foregrounds out of focus; we can use long shutter speeds to blur images, or very short ones to freeze movement; we can select unusual viewpoints from which to take ordinary pictures and render them less ordinary; with zoom lenses we can change the focal length during exposure; we can alter colors almost at will by using emulsions designed for light sources that are different from those under which we are photographing, or we can add colored filters to change the overall color. There are now available 'creative' kits that include just about every optical trick that can be used to make our pictures look 'different', and all these methods plus many others have their place, but if they are used indiscriminately they will simply result in gimmicky pictures; pictures with nothing to tell us; pictures which, without the gimmicks, we would throw away as worthless. No amount of technical manipulation can replace the ability to see and select; it can add a little 'something' to an already good picture but it should never be used as an end in itself. There seems to be far too much of a tendency, nowadays, to reach straight for the 'special effects' before we have fully considered and understood what it is about the subject that interested or excited us in the first place. There are exceptions, of course, and a considerable amount of commercial or commissioned photography comes into a category that demands a particular treatment, but in many cases, if we stop and ask ourselves exactly what it is about the subject that has made us stop and look, and then try to translate those feelings onto film in order to share the experience, then we will find that an honest and straightforward photograph that shows the light catching the subject in just that way, or at just that angle, with all our concentration on selecting the viewpoint and deciding what to include and, perhaps more important, what to exclude, then we will find that anything else is unnecessary; all that is required is careful photographic technique.

The task of choosing the photographs for this volume has been both enjoyable and immensely difficult. For each picture that was selected there were many, many alternatives and the overriding consideration has been variety: variety of pictures, of course, but also variety of technique. There are numerous ways in which a flower, a landscape or a girl can be photographed and no one way is necessarily the right way, or the best way. Despite what was written in the previous paragraph, there are photographs that display various forms of photographic tricks, for, it must be remembered, these are 'commercial' photographs; they have all either been used – some many times – or they are available for use, and different markets demand different types of pictures. It must be stated, however, that the compilers feel, most strongly, that every picture is worthy of its inclusion, on its own merit, in this collection. There has been no attempt to 'fill up space', on the contrary, many pictures had to be left out because there simply was not enough room for them in a book of this size. Whether the desired aim – of presenting some of the best color photography available – has succeeded or not is up to you, the reader, to judge.

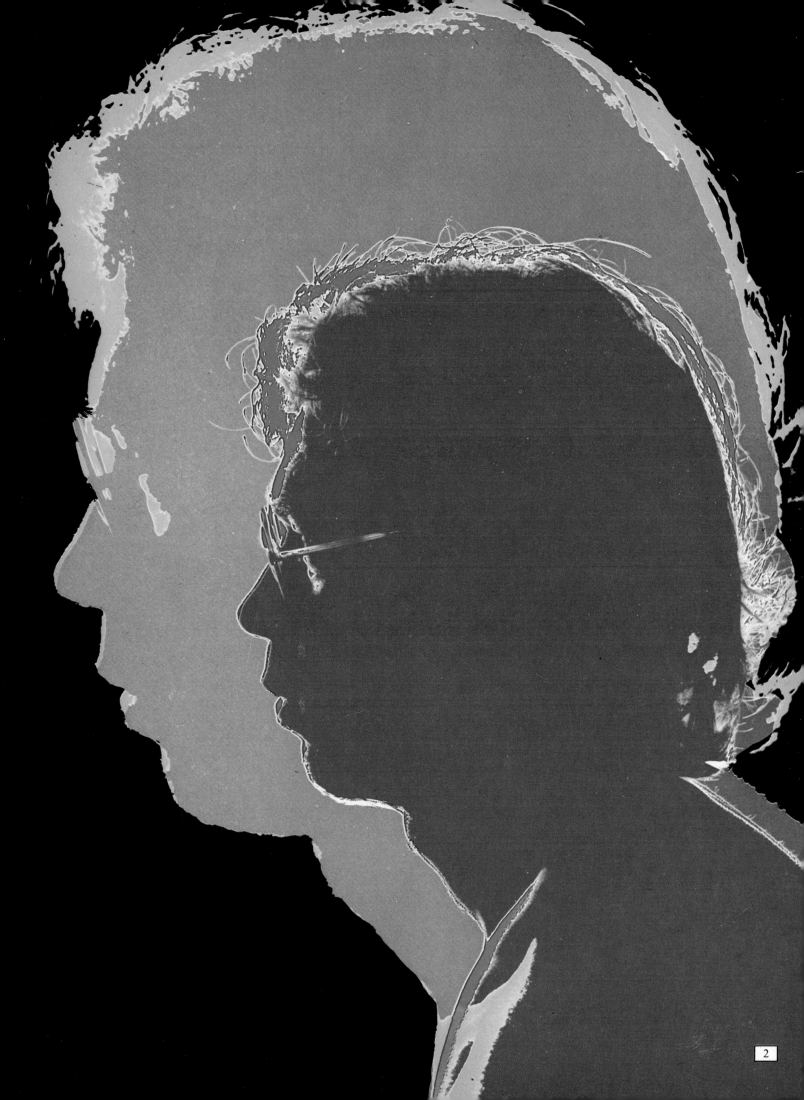

3

4

6

9

12

14

17

21

26

27

35

40

41

43

47

51

52

56

57

60

61

63

67

68

71

72

79

81

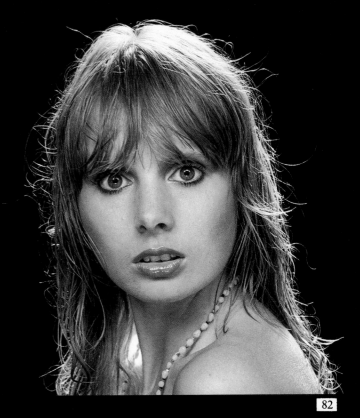

82

83

84

90

91

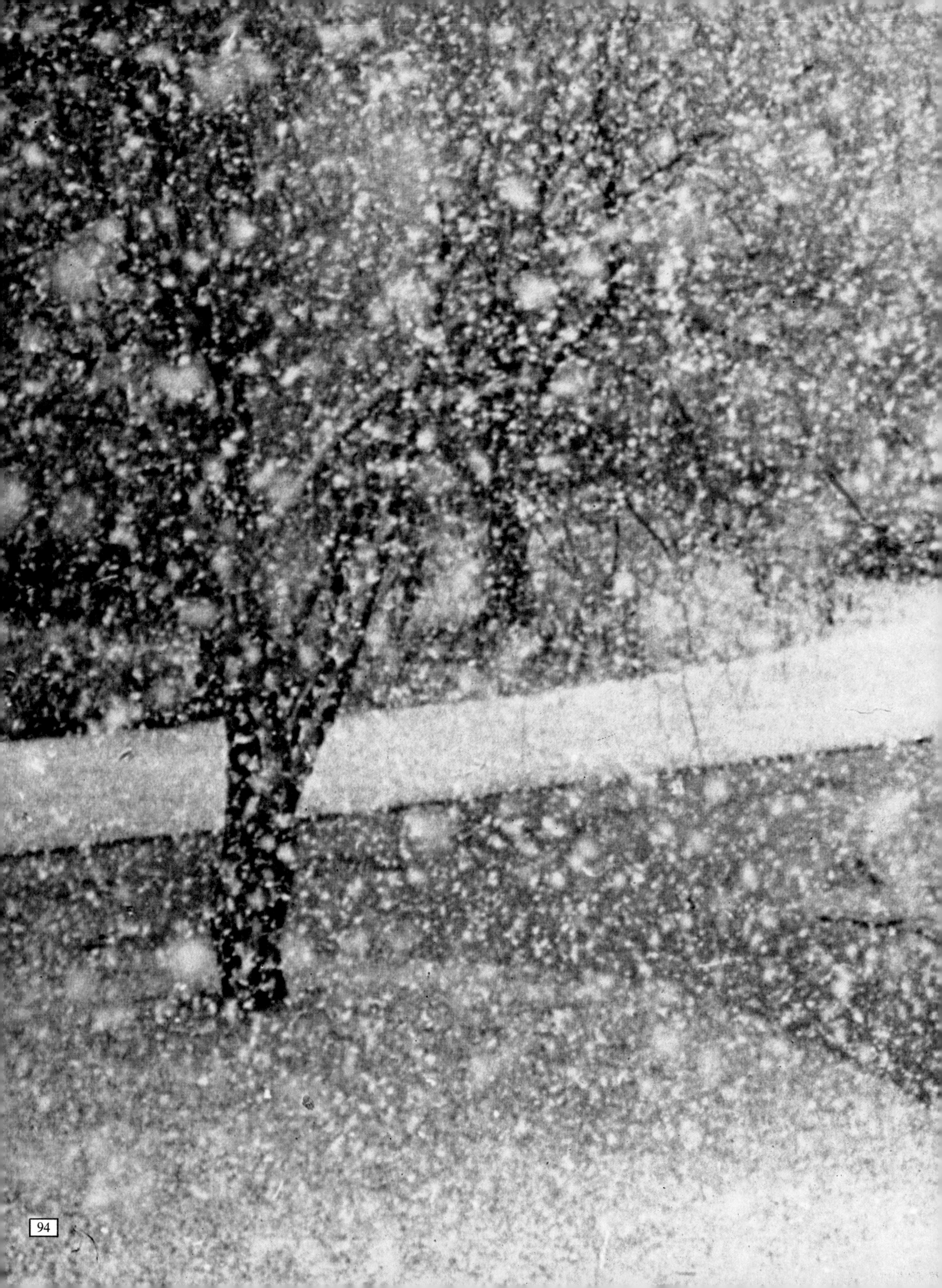

98

99.

103

104

105

106

114

115

118

119

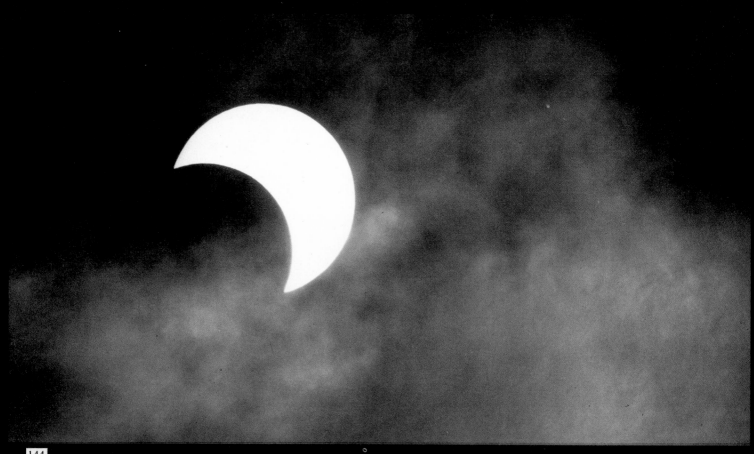

144

145

149

150

153

154

161

162

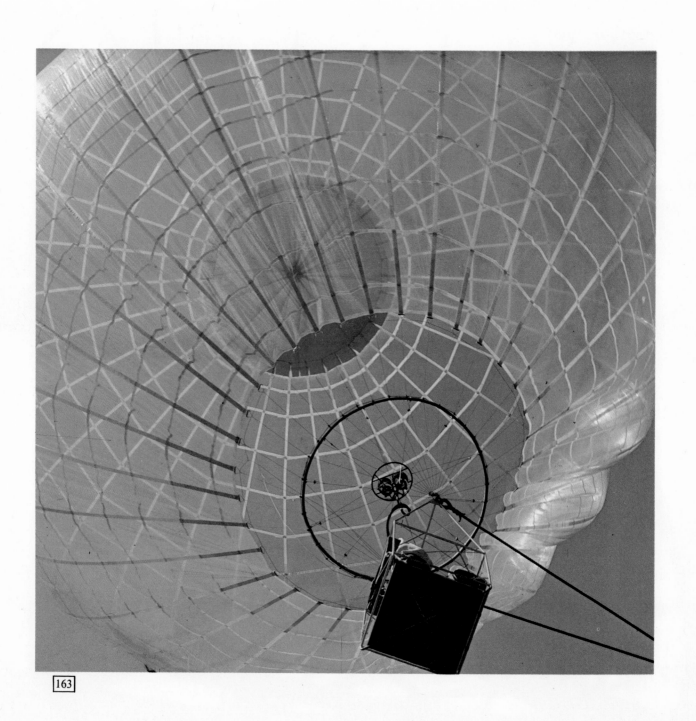

163

167

168

For the following technical details section we were able, in almost every case, to contact the photographers concerned so that accurate information could be provided regarding cameras, lenses and exposures. Obviously, busy photographers seldom keep notes on exact exposures other than in exceptional circumstances, but they do know the way they work and it is surprising how well they can recall almost all the details of a particular shot. In the few cases where photographers could not be reached we have made the comments 'No technical details available' or 'Not recorded'.

1. *Photographer:* Tom Hustler
    Camera: Rolleiflex twin lens reflex
    Exposure: Not recorded

A direct and startling portrait using equally startling make-up. Head on to the camera, the symmetry of the face is broken only by the black drapery.

2. *Photographer:* J. Vilanova

We were unable to obtain from the photographer any technical details regarding this particular picture, but there are several different ways in which this effect could have been produced. It will be noticed that there are two very slightly different images involved initially; both are head shots, in profile and back lit, in such a way as to provide high contrast between the background and the face. Using register pins on the baseboard, the image is then projected in an enlarger and positive and negative films are made, in sizes, according to the final result required. By using the positives, in position on the baseboard, various parts of the image can then be exposed through different colored filters. Each time an exposure is made, however, it must be subsequently covered by the appropriate positive in order that it is not re-exposed to another color. In this way a number of exposures in bold, strong colors can be made, but it must be emphasized that this is very much a subject for experimentation and the above is merely a brief outline of one method that can be used.

3. *Photographer:* Roy Day
    Camera: Gandolfi 10×8 inch
    Lens: 300mm Symmar
    Exposure: 1/30 at f16
    Film: Agfachrome 50 S

The old, wooden 10×8 cameras are seldom seen nowadays except in the studio, and even there they are becoming something of a rarity; 10×8 film is expensive, the slides – and cameras – are bulky and heavy to carry around and, of course, because of the large format, they offer very little in the way of depth of field. Nevertheless, this particular photographer has always worked outdoors with such cameras, and when asked to produce some 'soft' shots, with petroleum jelly smeared over a piece of glass held in front of the lens, this was the equipment with which he chose to do them. Interestingly enough, despite the degradation of the image, there is something about the shot that says 'large format' – the definition in the sharper parts of the picture and, most of all, the gradation of color in the flowers, partly due, not surprisingly, to the relatively small degree of enlargement necessary even to produce a print of this size.

4. *Photographer:* Neil Sutherland
    Camera: Arca-Swiss 5×4
    Lens: 180mm Symmar
    Exposure: 1/125 at f8
    Film: Agfachrome 50 S

The photographer carefully chose his angle in order to position the horses on the skyline. Carefully, it must be stressed, because, above all, he did not want to disturb them and have them running off to some distant corner of the field. There is inevitably a sense of urgency about trying to take a shot like this. In this case the horses were already exactly as the photographer wanted them in relation to each other, and there was the fear that at any moment one or other of them would move away. When making his exposure Neil chose to silhouette the horses against the sky, and in order to further suppress detail in the foreground and add drama to the sky he fitted an orange filter to the lens and chose a fairly fast shutter speed to freeze any sudden movement in the horses' tails.

5. *Photographer:* Edmund Nägele
    Camera: Pentax 6×7
    Lens: 105mm
    Exposure: Not recorded
    Film: Ektachrome

In the first place it must be said that this is but a small section from a 6×7cm transparency. Secondly, the picture is not exactly what it might seem. The two animals were noticed on the skyline and the possibilities of such a photograph were seen, so the photographer used one of the rolls of film he carries with him on which he had previously exposed discs of suns – either genuine or shot in the studio – for just such occasions. He knew, from notes he had made, the precise position of the pre-exposure and was, therefore, able to position the image just where he wanted it.

6. *Photographer:* Neil Sutherland
    Camera: Arca Swiss 5×4 monorail
    Lens: 180mm Symmar
    Exposure: 1/8 at f22
    Film: Agfachrome 50 S

The colors of fall used to create an all-over pattern that somehow suggests a waterfall. The problem with this type of shot is, having set the camera up in position – obviously on a very solid tripod – having to wait until there is barely a breath of wind to disturb the leaves and fronds during the relatively long exposure.

7. *Photographer:* Neil Sutherland
    Camera: Arca Swiss 5×4
    Lens: 180mm Symmar
    Exposure: 1/30 at f16
    Film: Agfachrome 50 S

Once the works of man are abandoned nature soon takes over again, sometimes until the very things that were an intrusion seem almost part of the natural order. Such is the case with this picture of early morning frost in Surrey. The rotting gatepost seems to belong, almost as much as the vegetation. One of the problems of working on subjects such as this on large format is having to carry a considerable amount of heavy equipment, including a very sturdy tripod, over rough ground, looking for subjects that are interesting and meet the brief that has been given.

8. *Photographer:* Neil Sutherland
   Camera: Pentax 6×7
   Lens: 55mm
   Exposure: 45 seconds at f16
   Film: Agfachrome 50 S

For this subject, the floodlit Herengracht at its point of intersection with the Reguliersgracht, Amsterdam, the photographer could have used a film balanced for artificial light – i.e. of a lower color temperature – which would have rendered the subject much bluer and more accurate. Under such conditions, however, the overall yellow and warmth of daylight film often gives a more pleasing result. Should any people, or unwanted vehicles, have passed through the frame while the exposure was being made, the photographer would have covered the lens until they had gone, and then uncovered it, adding the time it was covered to the time for the exposure.

9. *Photographer:* Edmund Nägele
   Camera: Pentax 6×7
   Lens: 105mm
   Exposure: 1 sec at f8
   Film: Ektachrome

By their very nature, subjects such as stained-glass windows (here at Canterbury Cathedral) require that light be transmitted through them for their full effect to be seen. Very bright sunlight, however, can cause contrast problems and many photographers prefer to wait for softer, indirect lighting conditions. A direct exposure reading can usually be employed, taking the lightest and darkest parts of the subject and either averaging out the results or favoring the most important parts of the window.

10. *Photographer:* Edmund Nägele
    Camera: Pentax 6×7
    Lens: 105mm
    Exposure: 1/125 at f16
    Film: Ektachrome·

This serene view was captured in Prince Albert National Park, Saskatchewan, Canada. The exposure has allowed the silhouette of the people in the canoe to be retained while overexposing the evening sun. A small aperture, with the lens exactly centred on the strong light source has caused the circular 'rainbow', rather than the use, as might be thought, of a 'special effect' fitment.

11. *Photographer:* Manfred Uselmann
    Camera: Hasselblad
    Lens: 80mm Planar
    Exposure: 1/125 at f16
    Film: Not recorded

All the ingredients for producing a strong, vibrant color composition are here: clear atmosphere, vivid primary colors and clean whites. With a subject such as this, from a reasonable distance, there are no apparent problems when the camera is tilted upward slightly to get rid of some of the foreground. In situations like this an ultra violet absorbing filter is practically essential and a polarizing filter can be very useful.

12. *Photographer:* Nick Meers
    Camera: Mamiya RB67 Pro S
    Lens: 50mm Mamiya Sekor
    Exposure: 1/2 at f5.6

Film: Agfachrome 50 S

Daylight film adds a mellow glow that enhances the atmosphere of this typical pub scene, which was shot in Bourton-on-the-Water in Gloucestershire. The shot was not set up and no tripod was available, so the bar served as a camera support.

13. *Photographer:* Neil Sutherland
    Camera: Pentax 6×7
    Lens: 105mm
    Exposure: 1/125 at f8
    Film: Agfachrome 50 S

On his way to an assignment in New York, the photographer saw this amusing cameo and simply shot what he saw.

14. *Photographer:* Will Curwen
    Camera: Pentax 6×7
    Lens: 300mm
    Exposure: 1/125 at f5.6
    Film: Agfachrome 50 S

The photographer's notes for this picture simply state: 'View of rocks and spray with rainbow, at foot of American Falls, Niagara Falls, New York State'. Rainbows are quite often seen where there is a fine mist, or spray, of water. Because they are delicate, overexposure lessens their effect, while exposure for the rainbow itself can result in underexposure of the rest of the picture. In this particular example, the balance is just about right.

15. *Photographer:* Edmund Nägele
    Camera: Pentax 6×7
    Lens: 105mm
    Exposure: 1/60 at f4
    Film: Ektachrome

Some pictures, simple though they may be, have an odd, almost mysterious quality. We may be quite happy with them, and like them, but we wonder what they are about and because we can find no obvious answers we sometimes find them slightly disturbing. This exposure was made in the late afternoon and a blue filter was used to deepen the blue of the sky and reduce all the other tones until the main subject was almost in silhouette.

16. *Photographer:* Edmund Nägele
    Camera: Pentax 6×7
    Lens: 55mm
    Exposure: 1/30 at f16
    Film: Ektachrome

Edmund Nägele spent a considerable time in America, photographing the National Parks, and it was while he was there that he saw this scene that seems to typify the American pioneering spirit; endless miles of railway track disappearing into the far distance, a lonely cabin and a 'big sky'.

17. *Photographer:* Manfred Uselmann
    Camera: Hasselblad
    Lens: For figures 80mm, for sun not recorded
    Exposure: Not recorded

This is a combination of two transparencies, which is fairly clear from the size of the setting sun in the background. Sandwiching a golden sunset with the figures has resulted in the overall yellow glow. An obvious point to watch with this type of picture is that the main light source should be in approximately the same position and from the same direction for both transparencies.

18. *Photographer:* See following explanation

Three different people were involved in the production of this picture. While the result has the appearance of a sandwich of transparencies, the principle involved is different. The photograph of the boys with fishing nets had a rather washed-out background and so it was decided to combine it with a flower close-up and add an overall color. The two transparencies were projected, in an enlarger, at different magnifications onto Ektachrome type 6121 duplicating film, and a magenta gel was used to add the color, transforming a rather ordinary picture into a commercially viable work.

19. *Photographer:* Clive Friend
    Camera: Sinar 5×4 with 6×9cm rollfilm back
    Lens: 135mm Symmar
    Exposure: 1/15 at f11
    Film: Agfachrome 50 S

India is a land rich in architectural subjects for the photographer. This particular example, with its almost countless curves, columns and angles, is of the Diwan-i-Am, in Agra's Red Fort. The low, evening sun has brought out the beautiful warm color in the stonework and the composition is exactly right. There are two separate halves to the picture: the right is quiet and tranquil, the receding columns and arches forming a perfect frame for the tree in the distance, and the left side is much busier, with its grouping of people in just the right position. The sun was setting quickly and there was little time to set up the camera, compose the shot, work out the exposure – bearing in mind that the moment had to be just right so as not to show movement in the group of people – before the light changed.

20. *Photographer:* Will Curwen
    Camera: Pentax 6×7
    Lens: 300mm
    Exposure: 30 seconds at f4

Churches and cathedrals are notoriously difficult places in which to photograph. Very often the light level is extremely low, and where there is light there are also heavy shadows, making contrast impossibly high unless extra lighting is brought in. This particular shot, however, makes use of the heavy shadows, the exposure only being for the altar and windows in, in this case, the Metropolitan Cathedral in Liverpool.

21. *Photographer:* Edmund Nägele
    Camera: Pentax 6×7
    Lens: 105mm
    Exposure: 1/60 at f16
    Film: Ektachrome

For this shot taken in Monument Valley, Utah, the photographer used a relatively short exposure to keep the silhouette effect and added a blue filter plus a special effects attachment to dramatise the sun.

22. *Photographer:* Tom Parker
    Camera: 6×6cm twin lens reflex
    Lens: 80mm
    Exposure: 1/60 at f5.6
    Film: Ektachrome

A peaceful scene that must be familiar to many people. The low, winter sun casts its warm, golden glow over tranquil Lake Windermere, Cumbria. The reflection of the tree has helped to fill in an otherwise empty foreground, and the swans add movement and interest.

23. *Photographer:* Nick Meers
    Camera: Nikon F2
    Lens: 28mm
    Exposure: 1/8 at f11
    Film: Kodachrome 64

These strange silhouettes were seen at Venice Beach, Los Angeles, by Nick Meers, who exposed only for the brightest part of the evening sky and selected a shorter lens than normal to include the depth of sky.

24. *Photographer:* Neil Sutherland
    Camera: Pentax 6×7
    Lens: 55mm
    Exposure: 1/30 at f16 – 2 Monolite 400 electronic flash heads with umbrellas.
    Film: Agfachrome 50 S

The items themselves in this Japanese meal – Hamani Bento – lend themselves to precise and elegant composition; even the food in the dishes is tastefully arranged. The photographer has done justice to his subject by using a black background and even, almost shadowless lighting, so that it is presented clearly and simply to the viewer.

25. *Photographer:* David James
    Camera: Hasselblad
    Lens: 80mm Planar
    Exposure: Not recorded
    Film: Not recorded

A carefully set up shot that required one primary and vital ingredient: the ability to see the possibilities in the shape and color of the window. There were, obviously, different things that could have been done; the model could have been dressed in contrasting colors or a subject other than a girl could have been used. Instead we have a perfect matching of tones and a striking, challenging photograph.

26. *Photographer:* Photri
    Camera: 35mm SLR
    Lens: Not recorded
    Exposure: Not recorded

Skiing events can always be relied on to produce exciting subjects. It must be remembered that the skiers will be traveling at very high speeds, and trying to change focus as a skier comes towards the camera can be extremely difficult. A better plan is, as here, to focus on one of the 'gates', to negotiate which the skier will have to change direction, thus slowing down and providing a spray of snow and ice as the skis 'bite' into their new course.

27. *Photographer:* Alexander Hubrich
    Camera: Pentax 6×7
    Lens: 150mm
    Exposure: 1/125 at f4
    Film: Agfacolor CT18

Timing is of the utmost importance in capturing sports subjects. In this particular shot, with this equipment, it is clear that the depth of field is very small. Very precise focusing and the peak of the action has resulted in a fine shot. Even the relatively high shutter speed, fast enough to catch some of the water droplets, has not completely frozen the action, so the impression of movement has still been retained.

28. *Photographer:* Alexander Hubrich
    Camera: Pentax 6×7
    Lens: 400mm

Exposure: 1/125 at f8
Film: Agfacolor CT18

As is evident from the blurred background, this is a panned shot. Providing focus is accurate and the subject is followed precisely, a relatively slow shutter speed will result in a sharp subject, and the blurred background adds to the impression of movement.

29. *Photographer:* Edmund Nägele
    Camera: Pentax 6×7
    Lens: 600mm
    Exposure: 1/500 at f11
    Film: High speed Ektachrome – uprated

The peak of the action in surfing usually takes place some way out from the shore, so a long lens is essential. Speeds can also be considerable as well as sudden changes of direction! For these reasons a fast shutter speed, and the smallest aperture possible – in order to cater for focusing-errors – are advisable, and this often means the use of a high speed film, uprated if necessary. This particular shot was taken during an assignment in Hawaii, shooting pictures for a book.

30. *Photographer:* Neil Sutherland
    Camera: Pentax 6×7
    Lens: 105mm
    Exposure: 1/2 sec at f11
    Film: Agfachrome 50 S

Although the whole of the subject, Rockefeller Plaza in New York splendidly decorated for Christmas, was illuminated by artificial light, the photographer chose to use a film that was balanced for daylight, which gives an 'incorrect' color rendition. This is because daylight film is intended for use in daylight, which is much bluer, and artificial light being much lower on the colour temperature scale, by as much as 2,000 degrees K., the use of daylight film under artificial lighting results in this typical 'yellow' cast. However, there are occasions, such as this, when the golden warmth is exactly what the photographer wished to convey. Conversely, artificial light film used in daylight will result in an overall blue cast. Again, there may well be instances when this is just what is wanted, and this is merely another control that the photographer has over the final result.

31. *Photographer:* Edmund Nägele
    Camera: Pentax 6×7
    Lens: 200mm
    Exposure: 1/125 at f11
    Film: Ektachrome

A very beautiful, and simple, study of a seagull. As anyone who has tried photographing these graceful birds will know, however, the subject is by no means as simple as it looks. The deep blue sky, with neither clouds nor other birds in sight, helps enormously, and this was, obviously, something over which the photographer had no real control other than in careful positioning and waiting until only the one bird was in frame. Unless the sun is very low, birds in flight are almost always seen against the light and while this can produce beautiful lighting it can cause problems unless, as here, the photographer is standing on light colored sand, or it could be a light colored path, so that sufficient light is reflected back into the underside of the bird.

32. *Photographer:* Edmund Nägele
    Camera: Pentax 6×7
    Lens: 105mm plus close-up tube

Exposure: 1/15 at f16
Film: Ektachrome

Ice crystals are a fascinating subject in themselves. Like snow flakes, no two formations of ice crystals are exactly the same. In this particular shot, the form they have taken echoes the shape of the seed head of the plant, and the combination makes an interesting pattern. The camera was tripod mounted, as it is in most of Edmund Nägele's work, whether large or small format, and it is with subjects such as this that the removable pentaprism comes into its own, doing away with the problem of having to get right under a camera which is already positioned at a low level.

33. *Photographer:* David Gibbon
    Camera: Nikon F
    Lens: 50mm
    Exposure: 1/60 at f8
    Film: Ektachrome X

A soft, gentle portrait of a very lovely girl, taken in Barbados. A soft focus attachment was used to further soften the image, and out of focus areas were also employed to emphasise this feeling. The technical details are simple but it may be interesting to mention that the assignment was primarily for the purpose of producing glamour and pin-up shots. Only an hour before this picture was taken, the model was posing in a bikini, mentally attuned to that particular type of picture. In addition to re-doing her hair and make up, the girl had to change her mental attitude, and the photographer spent some time talking to her about the idea he had in mind before this series could be shot and, hopefully, the dreamy quality that both he and the model were trying to achieve has been realized.

34. *Photographer:* David Gibbon
    Camera: Rollei 35 LED
    Lens: 40mm (non-interchangeable)
    Exposure: 1/60 at f11
    Film: Kodachrome 64

This is a good example of the type of picture that can be handled quite successfully by a relatively simple camera having a fixed lens and scale focusing. The possibilities of the picture were seen, as were the children, who were playing on another part of the beach. It was simply a matter of selecting a small aperture and pre-focusing, using the depth of field scale, to allow the greatest possible sharpness, from the nearest stones all the way to the top of the ridge, and being ready, when the children decided to climb the stones, to take the shot.

35. *Photographer:* Ron Oulds
    Camera: 5×4
    Lens: Not recorded
    Exposure: 1/8 at f22
    Film: Ektachrome

Fall colors at Fittleworth, Sussex. Bright sunlight in situations such as this can look very attractive but can also cause problems of contrast, whereas soft lighting lends a gentle, peaceful look to the scene. In order to achieve maximum depth of field the photographer used a small aperture which necessitated the use of a correspondingly slow shutter speed. This meant that, ideally, there should be no subject movement during the exposure, requiring that all parts of the picture had to be carefully watched until the moment seemed right.

36. *Photographer:* Mittet
    Camera: 5×4

Lens: 90mm
Exposure: 1/15 at f22
Film: Ektachrome

Ferns in a pine forest in Ullero, Norway. Sunlight filtering through the forest has lit the whole of the floor of ferns with soft light, and the delicate greens contrast with the stark, heavy columns of the tree trunks. A breeze was obviously blowing, moving the greenery during the exposure, causing the shimmering effect.

37. *Photographer:* Alexander Hubrich
    Camera: Nikon F2A
    Lens: 80-200 Zoom
    Exposure: 1/4 at f22
    Film: Kodachrome 25 – duped onto Ektachrome

For this technique a low level of lighting and/or a slow film is required. Stopping the lens right down to a small aperture then allows the use of a slow shutter speed. The camera must be mounted on a tripod and the subject – or where it is expected to be – focused at the longest zoom setting. As the shutter is opened the zoom control is moved back to the shortest focal length. All this requires practice in order to achieve the smoothness and timing necessary. The center of interest should be in the center of the frame and the more bright areas there are in the background the more 'streaking' will be apparent. This particular subject was duplicated onto Ektachrome roll film which had the effect of increasing the contrast.

38. *Photographer:* Pedro Volkert
    Camera: Hasselblad
    Lens: 50mm
    Exposure: 1/8 at f22
    Film: Ektachrome

All the elements in this picture were very carefully chosen to bring to fruition the visualized concept. The road, trees, verges on either side, even the sky, all appear to converge in the center of the picture – the target. The sky has been deepened by the use of a graduated filter to emphasize the dramatic impact and in the foreground squats the car – a Lamborghini – its appearance of power heightened by the use of a wide-angle lens, which both exaggerates the perspective and allows sharpness all the way through to the background, so that everything is sharp and precise, like the angles of the car's bodywork. Everything seems to be waiting for the moment that will send the projectile on its way.

39. *Photographer:* Neil Sutherland
    Camera: Pentax 6×7
    Lens: 55mm
    Exposure: 1/2 second at f16
    Film: Agfachrome 50 S

Neil Sutherland was based for a while in New York, shooting pictures for a book, and he particularly wanted to show some of the restaurant interiors in the city. Some restaurants lend themselves to photography rather better than others, but it would be hard to find a more attractive setting than at the Sign of the Dove, at 1110 Third Avenue, which is the subject of this photograph. It was taken in February, at midday, just before the restaurant opened to serve lunch and the only lighting that was used was natural; that flooding through the many skylights. He made several exposures; in this one he used the mirrors at the far end of the room to give a feeling of spaciousness, and managed to capture exactly the feeling and atmosphere of the place.

40. *Photographer:* Michel Folco
    Camera: Nikkormat EL
    Lens: 28mm
    Exposure: On automatic – not recorded
    Film: Kodachrome 25

A sudden rainstorm in Shafter, in Texas, sent the photographer scurrying for the shelter of his vehicle. Once safely inside he became interested in the view through the windscreen, with its distortions increased by the raindrops and, fitting a wide-angle lens to his camera, he focused on these raindrops, leaving the camera to work out the exposure.

41. *Photographer:* Michel Folco
    Camera: Nikkormat EL
    Lens: 28mm
    Exposure: On automatic – not recorded
    Film: Kodachrome 25 .

Miles of shifting, wind-sculpted sand cover almost four thousand acres in the desolate Monahans Sand Hills, where drifting dunes can reach heights of up to 70 feet. It was here that Michel Folco made this exposure, creating an almost abstract, surrealistic landscape. He used a wide-angle lens to emphasize the foreground ripples and selected a small aperture to give maximum depth of field, leaving the camera to work out the shutter speed.

42. *Photographer:* Nick Meers
    Camera: Mamiya RB67
    Lens: 127mm
    Exposure: 1/60 at f8
    Film: Agfachrome 50 S

A field of poppies in Israel, on a roadside near Jerusalem. Taken almost straight into the sun, the photographer has used the resulting degradation of the image to create an impression of the poppies under the bright sun, rather than providing a detailed record. Incidentally, poppies nearly always look best when photographed in backlighting, even when shot in close-up.

43. *Photographer:* Peter Barry
    Camera: Hasselblad
    Lens: 80mm – plus soft-focus attachment
    Exposure: 1/60 at f8
    Film: Ektachrome Professional

Shooting in such places as the West Indies, where the sun is fierce and the light can be harsh, it is a mistake to take models out during the middle of the day. They tend to screw up their eyes against the intense glare, and even if you succeed in avoiding this there will usually be heavy shadows to contend with. One solution is to shoot in the shade or, as in this example taken in Grenada, to place the model partly in the shade so that her face at least is not in direct sunlight.

44. *Photographer:* Beverley Goodway
    Camera: Mamiya RB67
    Lens: 127mm
    Exposure: Electronic flash plus umbrella reflectors
    Film: Ektachrome

Beverley Goodway specializes in glamor photography and has long mastered the use of studio electronic flash to achieve the results he wants. A simple pose against a light colored background has resulted in a very direct and challenging study.

45.	*Photographer:* Neil Sutherland
	Camera: Arca-Swiss 5 × 4
	Lens: 180mm Symmar
	Exposure: 1/30 at f11
	Film: Agfachrome 50 S

An old barn in Rutland County, Vermont, provided the subject for this study in design and texture. It was taken in the autumn, or fall, and the sun was, therefore, low enough even in the middle of the day to accentuate the textures, but not so low as to cause shadow patterns, and detract from the main pattern of the picture.

46.	*Photographer:* Neil Sutherland
	Camera: Arca-Swiss 5 × 4
	Lens: 180mm Symmar
	Exposure: 1/30 at f11
	Film: Agfachrome 50 S

The photographer saw this quiet, peaceful scene of the Sugar House, so typical of rural New England, at Johnson in North Vermont, during an assignment to photograph the renowned fall colors in that beautiful part of the U.S.A.

47.	*Photographer:* Neil Sutherland
	Camera: Arca-Swiss 5 × 4
	Lens: 180mm Symmar
	Exposure: 1/8 at f22
	Film: Agfachrome 50 S

Ferns, turned brown at the end of the year, and covered in frost, attracted the photographer to this pattern in nature. He was at the time using a 5 × 4 camera, so it was necessary to set this up, place it on a tripod and make the exposure. When working with large format equipment it is quite easy to decide not to bother with incidental subjects such as this, particularly in the cold weather when constantly setting up the camera can prove quite arduous.

48.	*Photographer:* David Gibbon
	Camera: Nikon FE
	Lens: 55mm Micro Nikkor
	Exposure: 1/60 at f8
	Film: Kodachrome 64

This picture relies entirely for its effect on lighting. It is interesting in that it is typical of the many subjects that are available almost everywhere and require only that we look with a 'seeing' or perceptive eye. Low sunlight hit the nasturtium leaves in only a few places, but where it did strike it revealed both an intensity of color and a sharp delineation of the structure of the leaves. The camera was on automatic and hand held, and provides a good example of the use of this type of camera when the main subject area is towards the edge of the frame, rather than in the central (exposure-reading) area. The frame was first centered on the most important part of the subject – the portion of leaf that was brightly lit – the memory lever was then pushed in, to hold the exposure reading, the camera re-positioned and the exposure made.

49.	*Photographer:* Mittet
	Camera: Sinar 5 × 4
	Lens: Not recorded
	Exposure: Not recorded
	Film: Ektachrome

Bright winter sunshine brings to life this rural scene taken in Norway. The snow is still fresh and clean on the branches of the trees and there are just enough dark areas, in them and in the wooden church, to provide contrasting accents.

50.	*Photographer:* Michel Folco
	Camera: Nikkormat EL
	Lens: 28mm
	Exposure: On automatic – not recorded
	Film: Kodachrome 25

Watching a typical outdoor café scene in one of Cairo's narrow streets, the photographer realized that the only way he could get the shot he wanted was by shooting from an upstairs window of the building opposite. He sought and obtained permission to do so and then saw, from his vantage point, the sleeping figure through the window. Very wisely, he decided to include the figure in the picture of the café and thus turned what would have been merely an interesting photograph into something much more. It is perhaps worth noting that this particular photographer works very happily with automatic cameras, in the belief that the less he has to think about the technicalities involved, the more he can concentrate on the telling picture.

51.	*Photographer:* Michel Folco
	Camera: Nikkormat EL
	Lens: 28mm
	Exposure: On automatic – not recorded
	Film: Kodachrome 25

At Giza, in Egypt, a tour guide beckons the members of his party. The photographer allowed the camera to work out the exposure for him, leaving him free to concentrate on the precise moment of exposure or, as Henri Cartier-Bresson calls it, 'the decisive moment'.

52.	*Photographer:* Neil Sutherland
	Camera: Nikon F
	Lens: 8mm Fisheye (plus built-in orange filter)
	Exposure: 1/125 at f8
	Film: For original – Kodachrome 64 – subsequently duped onto Ektachrome duplicating film, type 6121.

This picture is typical of the distortion created by the use of a 'fish-eye' lens, in this case fitted to a 35mm camera, the transparency being subsequently duped onto 5 × 4 film as the circular image is rather small to be shown to prospective clients. These particular lenses require care in use; with such a wide angle of view it is quite easy for the photographer to include parts of himself in the picture, and they should only be used occasionally; they give such a different perspective from that to which we are accustomed that pictures taken with them can easily appear gimmicky.

53.	*Photographer:* Edmund Nägele
	Camera: Pentax 6 × 7
	Lens: 105mm plus deep orange filter
	Exposure: Not recorded
	Film: Ektachrome

Faced with a fairly ordinary subject of ruined buildings against a low sun, the photographer decided to silhouette the main subject, added an orange filter to heighten the 'sunset' effect and stopped the lens right down to its smallest aperture, centering the main light source – the sun – which has produced the halos and radiating lines.

54.	*Photographer:* Philip Barker
	Camera: Nikon F2A
	Lens: 28mm
	Exposure: 1/125 at f11
	Film: Kodachrome 64

The West Indies, in this case Grenada, is noted for its

beautiful golden beaches, clear sea and sunshine. The sun is, however, particularly strong and can cause very heavy shadows on models' faces. For this shot, therefore, the photographer sensibly decided to get his model to lie down, thus making sure he had no such problem. The picture divides rather well into approximate thirds, with the blue sky broken by cloud formations, the sea by the boat, raft and swimmer and the clean, gold sand by the figure of the girl, all blending to achieve a restful quality and the sort of subject that is much in demand for holiday travel promotion.

55. *Photographer:* Nick Meers
    Camera: Mamiya RB 67
    Lens: 50mm
    Exposure: 1/125 at f11
    Film: Agfachrome 50 S

The aptly-named Paradise Beach, on Paradise Island in the Bahamas, was the exotic setting for this photograph. The picture is quite genuine, although the clarity of the water and the heavy, lowering storm clouds in the sky might lead one to suppose otherwise.

56. *Photographer:* Edmund Nägele
    Camera: Pentax 6×7
    Lens: 150mm
    Exposure: Not recorded
    Film: Ektachrome

A wet road and a very low sun provided the basic ingredients for this picture. The location was Seward Highway, near Anchorage, along Turnagain Arm, in Alaska, and the subject was completed by the appearance of a small car, which was photographed in just the right place to balance the picture.

57. *Photographer:* Edmund Nägele
    Camera: Pentax 6×7
    Lens: 600mm
    Exposure: Not recorded
    Film: Ektachrome

Although this picture, taken near Las Cruces, in Colorado, has a look of pioneer America about it; of wagons heading westward into the setting sun, it shows, in fact, nothing more unusual than trucks and cars on Interstate Highway 10. The photographer used a long lens both to compress the apparent perspective and to emphasize the size of the sun.

58. *Photographer:* Colin Glanfield
    Camera: Hasselblad
    Lens: 80mm
    Exposure: Not recorded
    Film: Ektachrome artificial light

This shot was taken simply because the idea appealed to the photographer. It was obviously a good idea because it has been used by several clients for different purposes. Most people who see it say it puts them in mind of something along the lines of a science fiction story; a sort of 'close encounter'. A night with a full moon was chosen and the car placed as if heading towards it. Another car was positioned, with headlights on, facing the camera but hidden from it by the nearer car.

59. *Photographer:* Edmund Nägele
    Camera: Pentax 6×7
    Lens: 105mm for main subject, 800mm for moon
    Exposures: Not recorded
    Film: Ektachrome

A musher and dog team on Iditarod Trail, near Nome, Alaska, form the subject for this picture, which beautifully illustrates the icy bleakness of life in this part of the American continent. The photograph was taken in daylight, with a watery sun in the position occupied by the moon in the finished result. Ed always carries with him a selection of previously exposed – and very carefully re-rolled – films of moon shots. This re-rolling is by no means easy to accomplish, and it additionally means that the film must be placed in the camera and wound on in exactly the same manner for the second exposure as it was for the first. Each pre-exposed film carries careful notes as to the position of the moon in various frames and, having loaded it into the camera, it is then necessary to position the camera so that the moon from the first exposure exactly coincides with the position of the moon – or in this case, sun – in the second exposure. Because this particular exposure was made in daylight, Ed added a blue filter to create the feeling of moonlight as well as the coloring. A point to note is that, when shooting in very low temperatures, battery voltage may drop or fail altogether. With cameras that depend on battery power for shutter operation this obviously renders the shutter inoperable. This was exactly the problem that faced the photographer in this location and it was necessary for him to make an urgent request for a remote battery container to be sent to him. This item consists of a battery compartment, which can be placed in a warm, inner pocket, and a cord fitted with a plug which fits into the camera, thereby restoring normal camera functions even in extreme conditions.

60. *Photographer:* Edmund Nägele
    Camera: Pentax 6×7
    Lens: 55mm
    Exposure: 1/30 at f22
    Film: Ektachrome

There is a fascination about sand dunes. Constantly changing patterns as the wind reshapes them provides almost endless variety, and they have the look about them of a frozen seascape. This picture, taken almost directly into the sun to emphasize the ripples, waves and texture, was made in Death Valley, in California.

61. *Photographer:* Edmund Nägele
    Camera: Pentax 6×7
    Lens: 55mm
    Exposure: 1/30 at f16
    Film: Ektachrome

Seemingly endless miles of ripening wheat near Lethbridge, Alberta, Canada provided the subject for this photograph. The photographer used a wide-angle lens on his camera, partly to indicate the enormous sweep of the area, and partly to render as much as possible of the subject, from foreground to background, sharply.

62. *Photographer:* Edmund Nägele
    Camera: Pentax 6×7
    Lens: 150mm
    Exposure: Not recorded
    Film: Ektachrome

In order that crops may be grown successfully, the huge tracts of land under cultivation in Alberta, Canada, require extensive irrigation and it was this that provided the subject for this particular photograph.

63. *Photographer:* David Gibbon
    Camera: Nikon FE
    Lens: 50mm

Exposure: 1/60 at f8
Film: Kodachrome 64

A hard, overnight ground frost had caused the formation of pronounced ice crystals on the dead stems of this riverside plant in Surrey, England. The photograph was taken fairly early in the morning and the watery sun, particularly at that time of the year, was still low, outlining the shape of the plant and highlighting the ice. It was this aspect that the photographer wanted to capture and so he shot into the sun and its reflection in the river, using part of the plant to obscure part of the reflection. The exposure, with the camera set on manual operation, was kept short to the point of underexposure.

64. *Photographer:* David Gibbon
    Camera: Nikon FE
    Lens: 43-86mm zoom – set at 43mm
    Exposure: 1/30 at f8
    Film: Kodachrome 64

An early January morning by the River Mole, near Esher in Surrey. The large tree on the right was used as a frame to hold and balance the iron railings and trees on the left and the frost-covered grass and twigs in the foreground added interest. The low sun provided illumination of a lower color temperature than that for which the film was balanced, thus producing the warm coloring except in the sky area. The camera was on automatic and, at the desired aperture of f8, indicated and provided the corresponding shutter speed.

65. *Photographer:* Peter Pugh-Cook
    Camera: Hasselblad
    Lens: 80mm
    Exposure: Electronic flash
    Film: Ektachrome

The photographer was intrigued by the various patterns made by the beautiful dress worn by this dancer in Puerto Vallarta, Baja California, in Mexico and waited until she produced the shape he wanted before making several exposures, employing a hand-held flash gun, with the result that we have exactly the right amount of illumination to show the dress to full advantage.

66. *Photographer:* Peter Pugh-Cook
    Camera: Hasselblad
    Lens: 80mm
    Exposure: 1/60 at f11
    Film: Ektachrome

Everything seems right about this picture. It was taken at the Hotel Playasol in Acapulco, Mexico, and shows the hotel's swimming pool, situated right next to the beach. The shape of the pool, the sun loungers placed around it, the combination of colors, all contribute towards making the picture, but it was up to the photographer to see the possibilities and choose his viewpoint with care so as to realize the composition.

67. *Photographer:* Neil Sutherland
    Camera: Pentax 6 × 7
    Lens: 55mm
    Exposure: 1/60 at f11
    Film: Agfachrome 50 S

In this shot of an office building in Chicago, the photographer, after taking the standard view he had been asked for, saw the possibilities of producing an abstract design and selected the ideal viewpoint and angle from which to do it, deliberately allowing the black areas to be underexposed, to increase the contrast and accentuate the pattern of light and dark.

68. *Photographer:* Edmund Nägele
    Camera: Pentax 6 × 7
    Lens: 105mm
    Exposure: 1/15 at f16
    Film: Ektachrome

Aspens in Colorado with their typical, silvery-grey trunks and black accents, have here been used very formally, to fill the frame so that we know nothing of their position or relationship to anything else in the area, the whole emphasis of the picture being on the abstract pattern they create.

69. *Photographer:* Clive Friend
    Camera: Sinar 5 × 4
    Lens: 180mm Symmar
    Exposure: 1/8 at f16
    Film: Agfachrome 50 S

The Taj Mahal, that exquisite shrine built by Shah Jahan in memory of his wife Mumtaz Mahal, has been the subject of countless photographs. When Clive Friend was in India recently, taking photographs for a book on the country, he determined to show it, in addition to the more usual way, in such a manner as to evoke the spirit of the place rather than just the look of it, beautiful as that most certainly is. Accordingly, he chose to use the columns of one of the pavilions of the Khas Mahal, overlooking the Jumna river, in which to frame his subject and added the figure of the girl on the left, both to balance the composition and to add an air of wistfulness to it, and made his exposure in the soft, golden light of evening, creating a memorable picture.

70. *Photographer:* David Gibbon
    Camera: Nikon F
    Lens: 55mm Micro Nikkor
    Exposure: 1/30 at f11
    Film: Kodachrome II

After a heavy rainstrom in Devon, the photographer saw this single fuchsia flower which happened to be fully lit against the dark background. The droplets of water were all picking up the light and so he selected the slowest shutter speed at which he felt he could hand-hold the camera, which allowed him to stop the lens down far enough for the highlights to form star patterns, and made three exposures as quickly as he could before the light changed and the moment was gone. With subjects such as this, even working with small apertures, there is very little depth of field because of the short camera to subject distances involved and it is best not to try to keep re-focusing the lens, but to set the focus once and then move the camera itself backward and forward slightly to achieve the final point of sharpness. Even the slightest breeze would have made the use of the slow shutter speed impossible.

71. *Photographer:* David Gibbon
    Camera: Nikon F
    Lens: 55mm Micro Nikkor
    Exposure: 1/60 at f11
    Film: Kodachrome X

One of the main enemies of the photographer working outdoors on close-up floral studies is a breeze – even the lightest. In order to obtain the depth of field necessary at such close distances, a small aperture is required and this, of course, means a relatively slow shutter speed, so even a slight wind can cause the subject to go out of focus or unsharp because of movement. This particular subject was lit from above and behind but the central area corresponded rather well with the measuring circle of the Nikon Photomic head, so the exposure was based on this reading. The water droplets were not the result of rain; the photographer used a watering can to produce them, to add interest to the picture.

72. *Photographer:* David Gibbon
    Camera: Bronica S2a
    Lens: 75mm Nikkor
    Exposure: 1/60 at f11 with + 2 close-up lens
    Film: Ektachrome Professional

As anyone who has tried it will know, photographing bees or hover-flies on flowers can be very frustrating. No sooner do you have the subject framed and in focus than the insect departs, usually for the flower next to the one you have selected! These little creatures also move very fast, and it is quite easy to end up trying to chase them from flower to flower – and they usually win! Probably the best method of approach, and the one that this particular photographer employs, is to select one flower that makes an interesting composition, and where bees are in the vicinity, and simply wait until one lands and take the shot. Whether or not a tripod is used is, of course, up to the individual photographer and how confident he or she feels holding the camera steady.

73. *Photographer:* Neil Sutherland
    Camera: Pentax 6 × 7
    Lens: 105mm
    Exposure: 1/125 at f8
    Film: Agfachrome 50 S

The photographer's brief with this picture was not to take an obvious shot of the model, but, rather, to try to evoke a mood. In order to do this he had the girl dress in white and chose a location where there were no intrusive colors, only the greens of the foliage. He used a square of magenta gelatine over the lens, which produced the overall color cast and also degraded the image slightly, giving the soft feeling he wanted. With this type of work it is quite useful to carry an assortment of different colored gelatines, not necessarily photographic, but the sort that can be purchased in art suppliers. They can be cut into 4 inch squares, a hole punched in the corner of each, and they can then be held together with a paper fastener so that they can be fanned out and a suitable color selected and simply held over the lens during exposure.

74. *Photographer:* Michael Boys
    Camera: Hasselblad
    Lens: Not recorded
    Exposure: Not recorded
    Film: Ektachrome

There are very few details available for this picture but it would appear that some form of diffuser was used to soften the image and that it was shot against the light. Any color present would have been picked up from the surroundings of the room in which it was taken.

75. *Photographer:* D. Frone
    No technical details available
    Film: Kodachrome II

London's Paddington Station at noon. Although no technical details are available for this picture, it seems fairly certain that a wide-angle lens was used and that the shot was made from a passenger bridge. In the days of steam trains, railway stations seemed always to be full of noise, smoke, steam and bustle and, although those days are now long past, stations still exert a fascination. The perspective usually allows for interesting compositions and, like airports, stations seem to have an air of expectancy; of journeys about to be embarked on. The aperture used for this shot must have been fairly small as is indicated by the depth of field. It may also be of interest to note that movement in the figures near the edges of the frame is most apparent even though they are not moving across the frame. This is because the lens, being a wide-angle, tends to look at them obliquely, so that they seem to be moving across the frame more than if they were positioned to the front of the camera.

76. *Photographer:* Alexander Hubrich
    Camera: Pentax 6 × 7
    Lens: 600mm
    Exposure: Not recorded
    Film: Agfachrome CT18

Scrambling, trials, cross country – all events such as these tend to be either very dusty in hot weather or very muddy in the wet. Both sets of conditions can produce interesting but, of course, quite different pictures. When the subject is moving towards, or away from, the camera, the effect of movement is minimized, but the attitude of both the participants in this shot still conveys action.

77. *Photographer:* Alexander Hubrich
    Camera: Pentax 6 × 7
    Lens: 300mm
    Exposure: Not recorded
    Film: Agfachrome CT18

Although there is very little subject movement evident in this picture, partly because a fairly fast shutter speed was used and partly because the direction of movement is towards the camera rather than across it, the attitude of the horses and riders, the eager expressions, and the way they are all leading strongly into the action, suggests power, speed and urgency, and the out-of-focus background helps to accentuate this feeling by isolating the bright reds of the jockeys.

78. *Photographer:* Edmund Nägele
    Camera: Sinar 5 × 4
    Lens: 180mm
    Exposure: 1/8 at f16
    Film: Ektachrome

A simple and idyllic setting by the banks of a river in Quebec, Canada, with autumn colors softened by weak sunlight and a smear of petroleum jelly around the edge of a piece of plain glass held in front of the lens to produce the softness.

79. *Photographer:* Mittet
    Camera: Linhof 5 × 4
    Lens: 180mm
    Exposure: 1/60 at f11
    Film: Ektachrome

At the right time of the year it is by no means difficult to find snow subjects in Norway. Nevertheless, all the elements seem to come together well in this picture of a rushing stream with vapor rising from the water, wooden houses with logs stacked for the winter and, most important of all in snow pictures, a fresh fall, with snow outlining the branches of the trees.

80- *Photographer:* Beverley Goodway
84. *Camera:* Mamiya RB67
    Lens: 127mm
    Exposures: All studio electronic flash
    Film: Ektachrome

Five superb examples of the type of work that has made
Beverley Goodway a glamor photographer whose pictures
are always in demand for many different publications. All
these photographs are evidence of the high level of skill the
photographer has attained in lighting his models,
establishing a rapport with them, choosing the right
accessories, posing them in the way that seems most
natural, and so on. It will be seen that Beverley likes
working with dark backgrounds and backlighting and also,
in some shots, uses a blower directed at the model's hair.
There is also a very direct look to his photographs. The girl,
in each case, is looking straight into the camera which, in
turn, means that she is looking straight at the viewer.

85. *Photographer:* David Gibbon
    Camera: Nikon F2A
    Lens: 43-86 zoom at 86mm setting
    Exposure: 1/60 at f5.6
    Film: Kodachrome 64

A cold January day at Richmond, in Surrey, when the River
Thames had flooded. The water was high enough for the
branches of some of the trees to touch its surface. The sun
was low and watery and the photographer moved around
his subject until the sun was in exactly the position he
wanted. The picture is, of course, very simple in itself; it
was merely a matter of seeing that bringing together the
two elements – the sun and the reflection of the trees –
would produce an interesting composition.

86. *Photographer:* Peter Beney
    Camera: Linhof Technika ½ plate
    Lens: 210mm Sironar
    Exposure: 1/4 sec at f22
    Film: Agfachrome 50 S

An ice-covered lake in the Botanical Gardens at Norfolk, in
Virginia provided the subject for this wintry shot. The light
was poor but, the weak sun's reflection illuminated the ice
on the lake and meant that the plant life could be
silhouetted to create an interesting picture. It is surprising
how often, when conditions for photography are far from
ideal, a picture can be produced from almost nothing. This
is one of the major differences in approach between the
amateur and the professional: the amateur can simply
decide not to shoot, whereas the professional feels he
should justify his time and will look for some means of
taking a useful subject.

87. *Photographer:* Guy Withers
    Camera: Gandolfi Studio (specially constructed
        incorporating extra-long bellows)
    Lens: 480mm Rodenstock Apo-Ronar
    Exposure: Electronic flash
    Film: Ektachrome 1/1 plate – (8½ × 6½ ins)

Animal photography in the studio, particularly on large
format, is a highly specialized business. The depth of field
at a given aperture, at close distances, that a large format –
8½ × 6½, or 10 × 8 ins – camera allows is minimal. In order
to achieve a workable depth, very small apertures need to
be used, plus camera movements that allow the back of the
camera and the lens panel to be tilted in relation to each
other, to effectively provide rather more depth of field at
each stop. All this is difficult enough with still life subjects,
but when we introduce animals, with which we can have

only limited communication, then we really increase the
problems. It is no good trying to explain to an animal the
reasons for wanting it to stay in one position; if it feels like
moving it will do so! There are also sets to be considered.
These have to be constructed in the studio, to resemble, as
near as possible, outdoor locations. Everything has to be lit;
the sky background, the grass and flowers, and the
animals, as naturally as possible. Despite the problems,
there is a continuing market for this type of work and there
is no doubt that being able to place in front of a client
photographs of this subject on large format can make a big
difference to sales. Patience, and an understanding of, and
sympathy for, animals are obvious prerequisites for this
work. Guy Withers has long been a master of it and has
built up his skills over the years. He uses electronic flash, of
course, but it is interesting to note that he also employs,
particularly when shooting kittens and cats, a fairly
powerful tungsten lamp to prevent the animals' pupils
opening wide and producing a 'dead' look. The tungsten
lamp has no effect on the final exposure, being far less
powerful than the flash equipment used.

88. *Photographer:* Guy Withers
    Camera: Gandolfi Studio (specially constructed
        incorporating extra-long bellows)
    Lens: 480mm Rodenstock Apo-Ronar
    Exposure: Electronic flash
    Film: Ektachrome 1/1 plate – (8½ × 6½ ins)

A very appealing shot of equally appealing kittens taken in
the studio. With this kind of subject it would be quite
pointless to position the animals and then start fiddling
about with lights, exposure meters, camera positions or
anything else. Everything – the setting, background,
desired position of the subject, or subjects, lighting, camera
position, focus and exposure has to be finalized before the
animals are placed where they are wanted. Sometimes it is
a good idea to play with young animals before shooting
starts. This can help to create trust and interest, and it can
also serve to tire the, in this case kittens, to the point where
they are quite willing to remain relatively still and are no
longer too interested in investigating their surroundings.
Even so, there is a strong likelihood that many attempts
will have to be made before the little animals are in the
required position. At just the right moment the kittens'
attention has been caught; a fairly strong tungsten light has
ensured that their pupils are not wide open, and the shot is
made.

89-93.

These five pictures have been grouped together under the
heading of, for want of a better term, 'Color Graphics'.
There are several different ways of producing, in the
darkroom, effects such as these. The original can be a
transparency or a negative, either black and white or color.
The principle consists of making, from the original, three,
four or more negatives on high contrast black and white
film, varying the exposure from under to over, so as to
record on one film the highlight detail, on another the
middle tones, and on another the shadow detail. These
'separation negatives' can then be used as they are, or
re-copied onto positive film, and exposures made from
them onto color sensitive paper or film, introducing various
colored filters, one for each film and exposure, so as to
build up a final picture in which the highlights can be
recorded as one color, the shadows another, and the middle
tones yet another. The possibilities are almost endless and it
is necessary to experiment in order to achieve a pleasing
effect. When doing this it is wise to keep a careful detailed
record of each stage, otherwise a particular effect will be

impossible to repeat at a later time. Two or more different originals can, of course, also be combined to create abstract or surrealist images.

94. *Photographer:* Peter Lane
    Camera: 35mm SLR
    Lens: Not recorded
    Exposure: Not recorded
    Film: Ektachrome

A sudden snowstorm of almost blizzard-like intensity in Shepherds Bush, London, transformed a fairly ordinary scene into an almost abstract pattern. Obviously a slow shutter speed was not used, otherwise the snow would have been seen as streaks rather than regular blobs, and a small aperture was unnecessary as it would be almost impossible to achieve anything approaching real sharpness under such conditions. Everything, therefore, has been directed towards showing the conditions and the pattern, and the fortuitous appearance of the woman out walking her dog has supplied the finishing touch.

95. *Photographer:* Peter Pugh-Cook
    Camera: Hasselblad
    Lens: 80mm
    Exposure: 1/60 at f4
    Film: Ektachrome

Very late evening sun in Minorca provided just the right level and angle of illumination to light the face of the model. The photographer quickly realized the possibility of a shot and placed the girl against the dark doorway to produce a striking and subtle color composition. The picture well illustrates the fact that it is not necessary to have strong colors to produce a striking color picture.

96. *Photographer:* David Gibbon
    Camera: Nikon F
    Lens: 105mm
    Exposure: 1/60 at f8
    Film: Ektachrome X

One of a series of pictures taken at the Sandy Lane Hotel in Barbados. The brief was to shoot pictures of romantic couples. The weather was rather overcast and the photographer happened to see two of the models walking across the outdoor dance floor. Realizing that there was a picture there for the taking, he climbed a low balcony to make his exposures. The whole subject was predominantly light toned, so he used a pale blue gelatine filter over the lens to produce an almost monochrome picture, including the empty tables and chairs to accentuate the feeling of isolation when two people have eyes only for each other.

97. *Photographer:* Clive Friend
    Camera: Olympus OM1
    Lens: 24mm
    Exposure: Not recorded
    Film: Kodachrome 64

At Benares, in India, there is a long and celebrated line of bathing ghats and it was the collection of people gathered there one morning that prompted Clive Friend, who was shooting pictures for a book on India, to take this colorful and incident-filled shot. He wanted to show something of the area rather than concentrating on a few individuals, and he chose, therefore, a wide-angle lens, tilting it downwards to include as many people as possible in the foreground while still showing the river receding into the distance.

98. *Photographer:* Edmund Nägele

Camera: Nikon F
Lens: 50mm
Exposure: 1/250 at f11
Film: Kodachrome 64

Even a fast shutter speed was not sufficient to 'freeze' the water droplets in this shot completely, which is all to the good. The action is still obvious and the whole subject suggests exuberance and joy. Water droplets are usually seen to their best advantage when backlit and the girl, being in silhouette and completely anonymous doesn't detract from the picture in any way.

99. *Photographer:* Edmund Nägele
    Camera: Pentax 6×7
    Lens: 55mm
    Exposure: 1/15 at f16
    Film: Ektachrome

Having spent some time in Fort Steele Historic Park, in Vancouver, taking pictures for a book on Canada, Edmund Nägele was looking for a new angle on a much photographed subject. Heavy storm clouds were gathering, providing a dramatic backdrop to some of the still brightly lit old buildings. He decided to make use of the sky, and to further suggest the pioneering spirit of the place he framed his picture between the wheels of one of the wagons. A low viewpoint was obviously essential and it is at times like these that the value of a detachable viewfinder is most noted. Removing the prism finder, he was able to view the image from above and produce a strikingly different picture.

100. *Photographer:* Pedro Volkert
     Camera: Hasselblad
     Lens: 80mm
     Exposure: See details
     Film: Ektachrome

In order to produce this fashion shot, Pedro Volkert used a combination of techniques. For the background he employed a front projection system; for the streaks of colored light three hand lamps were taped together and different colored filters were fixed over them. Then, with the front projector switched off, they were moved across the picture area to create a secondary image. Following this the model was photographed, lit by a studio flash unit – Broncolor – which superimposed her image over the other two.

101. *Photographer:* Edmund Nägele
     Camera: Pentax 6×7
     Lens: 105mm
     Exposure: 1/8 at f11
     Film: Ektachrome

Heavy mist in Lady Bird Johnson Grove, Redwoods National Park, California. There is an eerie feeling about woods and forests in these conditions; the trees, their tops lost in the mists, seem to loom even larger than usual, and direction becomes confused. It is such conditions, however, that can be used to provide interesting pictures. Edmund Nägele set up his camera in just the right position to show where the sun would be likely to burn its way through the mist; but here he used a little trickery. He made his exposure on a film on which he had previously exposed shots of the 'sun'. The film had notes attached indicating the precise position occupied by the 'sun' and he was, therefore, able to position it exactly where he wanted it. The reason for the quotes around 'sun' are that, in fact, in this particular case it was created by nothing more than a torch shone through a hole in a piece of black card, which the photographer managed to photograph in his mobile camper, at night.

102- *Photographer:* Kenneth Beken
108. *Camera:* Hasselblad
Lens: 80mm
Exposure: All pictures 1/250-1/500 at f8
Film: Ektachrome

When Kenneth Beken, who specializes in producing top-quality yachting and racing pictures, was asked for some technical details and comments on this set of photographs, he considered it of the utmost importance to mention that the first priority in taking such pictures was not to get in the way of the competitors or in any way to interfere with the racing. This is equally valid advice for many types of photography, but particularly of sporting events. People will always co-operate with you in helping to get the best set of pictures possible when they know that you will co-operate with them and have an understanding of their priorities. Kenneth Beken uses a high speed launch from which to shoot his pictures and Hasselblads fitted with 80mm lenses on which to take them. He always fits UV filters over the lenses, primarily to protect them from the highly corrosive properties of sea water – a hazard that has equally adverse effects on electrical contacts, which precludes his use of motor driven cameras. Keeping horizons horizontal is vitally important and this is by no means an easy matter when you are shooting from a launch, perhaps in choppy seas, and concentrating on framing, focusing and waiting for the right lighting conditions, full sails and interesting action.

109. *Photographer:* Edmund Nägele
Camera: Pentax 6×7
Lens: 300mm
Exposure: Time exposure, details not recorded
Film: Ektachrome

Lightning in the evening sky over Ute Mountain, Cortez, Colorado. A lightning flash lasts for only a brief moment, so there is obviously little point in waiting for one to appear and then trying to photograph it. When a storm is raging, as here, the best method is to direct the camera towards the scene of greatest activity – tripod mounted, of course – close the lens down to an appropriate aperture depending on the conditions, but bearing in mind that the actual flashes, because of their intensity, will always be exposed, and open the camera shutter on 'time'– or set it to 'B' and hold it open with a locking cable release – and wait until one, or several flashes of lightning take place within the frame area.

110. *Photographer:* Knut Vadseth
Camera: Hasselblad
Lens: Not recorded
Exposure: Not recorded
Film: Ektachrome

Although no technical details were supplied for this charming little picture, taken in Norway, it is clear that a slow shutter speed must have been used, probably in the region of a quarter of a second or longer, in order to show the movement of the water. In this case the camera would have to be tripod mounted, or at least supported in some way. From the size of the leaves on the rocks it will be seen that this was a very small stream, and it is often the case that, when shooting in woods and fields, it pays to examine the small details rather than concentrating only on the landscape around us.

111. *Photographer:* Edmund Nägele
Camera: Pentax 6×7
Lens: 200mm plus extension tube

Exposure: 1/250 at f5.6
Film: Ektachrome

Flowers growing by the roadside in Colorado. In order to produce a soft picture, the photographer used a soft focus attachment and a fairly wide aperture. The resulting shot has, therefore, a degree of sharpness about it but the colors have spread.

112. *Photographer:* David Gibbon
Camera: Nikon F
Lens: 55mm Micro-Nikkor
Exposure: 1/60 at f8
Film: Ektachrome X

The photographer was taking pictures of close-ups of flowers when he noticed this butterfly which had just landed on some nearby blooms. He had time only to change position, reframe and shoot before the butterfly flew away. Inevitably, work of this nature demands that the lens to subject distance is quite short, and this creates problems. Suddenly moving the camera – and yourself – quite close to the creature, whether it is a butterfly or a bee, can cause it to react by flying away; on the other hand any undue delay can also mean that the prey has gone before the camera is in position. Short of working in the studio, there is no real answer to these difficulties other than patience, and yet more patience.

113. *Photographer:* Michel Folco
Camera: Nikkormat EL
Lens: 28mm
Exposure: On automatic – not recorded
Film: Kodachrome 25

A beautiful little scene of a teacher and pupils that the photographer chanced on while shooting an assignment in Egypt. Whether or not he found them as they appear, in this very attractive grouping, is not known, but it is likely that he may have rearranged them against the high, open window.

114. *Photographer:* Jean-Paul Paireault
Camera: Nikon F
Lens: 28mm
Exposure: Not recorded
Film: Kodachrome 25

There are still some places in the world where pictures can be taken that have a timeless quality. This photograph of camel riders and the Mycerinus pyramid in Egypt falls into such a category. It could have been taken yesterday, twenty or even a hundred or more years ago – had today's equipment been available – and it would probably look exactly the same. Silhouetting the elements of the picture has helped in this feeling; the picture tells us what we wish to know without any details – only shapes.

115. *Photographer:* Michel Folco
Camera: Nikkormat EL
Lens: 28mm
Exposure: On automatic – not recorded
Film: Kodachrome 25

The setting Egyptian sun turns everything to dark shapes against the yellow and gold dust and sand. Exposing for detail in the figures of the people and animals would have destroyed the feeling of this shot, resulting in a fairly ordinary, straightforward record, so the photographer decided to concentrate only on the atmosphere.
In conditions such as these the main enemy is dust and sand. The camera and lenses should be protected at all

times except when actually shooting and all the equipment should ideally be thoroughly cleaned and examined after each day's work.

116. *Photographer:* Alexander Hubrich
   Camera: Pentax 6×7
   Lens: 300mm
   Exposure: 1/500 at f4
   Film: Agfachrome CT18

In this shot of motorcycle scrambling, or cross-country racing, the photographer has chosen the ideal viewpoint. The camera was set up on a tripod and the lens focused on a point just this side of the crest of the hill. The rest was anticipation and experience. The riders often wear brightly-colored clothing, which adds to the color impact of the shot, but the main aim is to show speed and action. The rider would be invisible to the photographer as he came up the far side of the hill and so the right moment would be judged by either listening to the sounds of the bike's engine, having someone keep a lookout and signalling, or by using a remote control attachment to trigger the exposure. Whichever method is adopted, pressing the shutter at exactly the right moment, a fraction of a second before the peak of the action is reached, is all-important. Even a motor drive (not available for this particular camera) can miss the telling shot, and the photographer's experience and anticipation is usually considered more reliable.
Many sports photographers, in fact, use their motor drives on single shot, using them only to advance the film, in the same way as an auto-winder, leaving them free to concentrate on the precise moment to make the exposure.

117. *Photographer:* Marcus Brown
   No technical details available
   Film: Ektachrome

It would be hard to think of a more ideal setting for a subject such as this. A forest in summer with the sunlight filtering through the trees and a girl dressed in white, riding a white horse. The photographer chose a position where the track angled across the picture area and towards the camera position and where dappled shadows and bushes supplied foreground interest. He then waited until the horse and rider were precisely where he wanted them – in the center of the band of sunlight – and produced a picture which is both pleasing and peaceful.

118. *Photographer:* John Hinde
   No technical details available

A seemingly endless sea of greenery with accents of red as tea pickers go about their job on a tea plantation in Kenya.

119. *Photographer:* Ron Winwood
   Camera: Pentax SP500
   Lens: 135mm
   Exposure: 1/60 at f8
   Film: Ektachrome

Plowing in Norfolk. Birds – in this case seagulls – soon gather in considerable numbers when plowing is taking place. The obvious attraction is the newly-turned earth and all the grubs, insects and worms that are suddenly brought to the surface. The angle and the composition of this particular picture is attractive in itself but it has certainly been brought to life by the inclusion of the flock of gulls.

120. *Photographer:* Edmund Nägele
   Camera: Pentax 6×7
   Lens: 200mm plus 2× converter
   Exposure: 1/30 at f16
   Film: Ektachrome

A farmworker and tractor in Coldstream Valley, near Lumby, British Columbia, Canada. The composition of this subject is interesting. Approximately two thirds of the area is occupied by the massed fir trees on the slope in the background, but this is balanced by the relative busyness of the bottom one third, in which there are bands of green and brown balanced, again, by the uprights of the fencing and the trees and the red accent of the tractor.

121. *Photographer:* Beverley Goodway
   Camera: Mamiya RB67
   Lens: 127mm
   Exposure: Electronic flash
   Film: Ektachrome

The electronic flash equipment used in studios is normally equipped with modeling lights – ordinary light bulbs – which allow a visual check to be made on the effect that will be achieved with the flash. Without modeling lights it is extremely difficult to assess the density of shadows and highlights and the balance of light between the main subject and the background. In order to achieve the softness that is apparent in this shot the flash heads are usually reflected into silvered umbrellas or onto white polystyrene flats.

122. *Photographer:* Beverley Goodway
   Camera: Mamiya RB67
   Lens: 127mm
   Exposure: Electronic flash
   Film: Ektachrome

Although the lighting in this shot is basically soft – there are no hard shadows – the photographer has managed to produce a very direct and challenging portrait adding, by way of an incongruous touch, the heavy, studded collar and chain. The value of expertly-applied make-up is apparent in photographs such as this, where every detail of the girl's features can be clearly seen and examined.

123. *Photographer:* Edmund Nägele
   Camera: Sinar P
   Lens: 150mm
   Exposure: Not recorded
   Film: Ektachrome

Vancouver skyline at night. Faced with a subject like this – a city skyline at night, seen across a wide expanse of water – there are several ways in which it can be tackled. The usual method would be to compose the subject using the skyline and its reflection in the water as the main theme and to position the line of buildings so that it, and its reflection, filled the bottom part of the picture area with an expanse of sky above; or to position the interest at the top of the frame, in which case there would be an area in the foreground that would be empty of interest. The photographer, in this case, decided to position the center of interest at the top of the frame, but also decided to fill the foreground with color and interest, so as to produce a shot that was out of the ordinary. The method is fairly straightforward and requires a shutter equipped with a 'time' setting, or a locking cable release, and a tripod fitted with a center column that can be raised or lowered by means of a crank. Having set up the shot and calculated the exposure necessary, the shutter is locked open for the length of time required, at the end of which, instead of closing the shutter, the camera is lowered – (remember that the image is upside-down at the film plane) – smoothly and steadily until the main image is off the edge of the frame, and then the shutter is closed. Don't stop the camera, however, and then close the shutter – this will result in a secondary image. The slower the camera is lowered, the brighter will be the 'streaking', while moving the camera quickly will result in a fainter image. Remember that smoothness of movement is the secret.

124. *Photographer:* Edmund Nägele
   Camera: Pentax 6×7
   Lens: 105mm
   Exposure: 1/30 at f11
   Film: Ektachrome

In Colorado, where he was carrying out photographic assignments, including taking pictures in the Grand Mesa National Forest, Edmund Nägele saw this rather attractive grouping of aspens with light filtering through from the left, and placed his model in the foreground, softening the image as much as possible to produce a dreamlike feeling. There is a variety of ways in which this softening can be created, including different types of diffusion attachments, softars and the like, allowing light to flare into the lens, and, of course, the old standby, petroleum jelly smeared onto a square of clear glass placed over the lens.

125. *Photographer:* Neil Sutherland
   Camera: Arca-Swiss 5×4
   Lens: 180mm Symmar
   Exposure: 1/60 at f5.6
   Film: Agfachrome 50 S

In order to create this essentially high key flower study the photographer made sure that most of his main subject was either white or light colored, pegged his exposure to overexpose as much as he dared without obviously burning out all the detail in the flowers and added a center spot attachment to cut down detail in the surrounds of the pictures. Center spot filters – or, more correctly, attachments, are usually produced by either combining a distorting lens, often a close-up lens, with a clear glass central area, or a flat glass marked to produce a strong 'softar' effect, with a central area actually cut out. The effect is very much the same and the same result can be achieved by taking a piece of clear gelatine and lightly sandpapering it before cutting out a central portion by means of a pair of engineer's dividers, scribing the circle again and again until the gel is cut through.

126. *Photographer:* Peter Beney
   Camera: Hasselblad
   Lens: 50mm
   Exposure: Not recorded
   Film: Ektachrome

Within the spacious chamber of the Lincoln Memorial stands this marble sculpture of the man himself, carved by Daniel Chester French. At nineteen feet high, the statue presents a problem if you want to photograph it on its own rather than in its setting. Even with a wide-angle lens, if you keep the camera level and go back until you have the top of the statue in frame, you will find that you have too much foreground. The only answer, unless you have a perspective control lens, which has movements whereby the lens axis can be shifted off-center, rather like the rise and fall front standard of a view camera, is to tilt the camera upwards as has been done here.

127. *Photographer:* Douglass Baglin
   Camera: Rolleiflex
   Lens: 80mm
   Exposure: 1/8 at f16
   Film: Ektachrome

The aptly-named Desert of Pinnacles, Lancelin, Western Australia provided the subject for this photograph. The sun was very low, as may be judged from the length of the shadows, and it was these as much as the sentinel-like pinnacles, their golden glow, and the strange color of the sky that attracted the photographer. The ripples in the sand have been picked out well by the low lighting, creating a texture that adds interest to a strangely brooding picture.

128. *Photographer:* Gilbert Uzan
   Camera: Nikon F2A
   Lens: 105mm
   Exposure: 1/60 at f8
   Film: Kodachrome 25

This splendid picture, so typical of the man, is of Pope John Paul II and was taken during his historic visit to Poland. Without working through an agency that can obtain a quota of press cards, photographing personalities on official visits such as this one is very hard indeed. Unless you can get a good position, or simply be lucky enough to have chosen the right spot, then the only alternative is to shoot from some way back, with the longest lens you can lay your hands on, and preferably from a high vantage point.

129. *Photographer:* Bernard Hermann
   Camera: Nikon F2
   Lens: 300mm
   Exposure: Not recorded
   Film: Kodachrome 25

The Statue of Liberty, at the entrance to New York Harbor, must surely qualify as one of the most-photographed subjects in the world. So much so that it is no longer necessary to show it in any detail for it to be immediately recognizable; its outline, or silhouette, as in this very telling photograph, is enough to evoke the spirit of New York, and the huge ball of the sun and its reflection in the water add interest to a beautifully seen and executed shot.

130. *Photographer:* David Gibbon
   Camera: Nikon F
   Lens: 43-86 zoom
   Exposure: 1/60 at f16
   Film: Ektachrome X

A late afternoon shot in Barbados, in the West Indies. The couple were positioned against the light reflected in the water, with enough space between them so that, with the lens closed down to a small aperture, the highlights recorded as star patterns. A medium blue filter (gelatine) was added to increase the blue of the water and accentuate the romantic feeling of the shot.

131. *Photographer:* David Gibbon
   Camera: Nikon F
   Lens: 105mm
   Exposure: 1/125 at f8
   Film: Ektachrome X

After taking numerous couple shots on location in Barbados the photographer wanted to produce something a little different. He also wanted to show the couple, but not in a way where they could be recognised. He used backlighting, catching the sparkling highlights in the water, and, from the collection of gelatine squares he always carries with him when shooting, he selected a yellow, an orange and a green and held the corners of all three in front of the lens while he took his pictures. The results using this method are fairly predictable, given experience, although it is difficult to duplicate a shot exactly.

132. *Photographer:* Photri
   No technical details available

'OH-6A helicopters in echelon formation at sunset' is the only information the photographer supplied with this picture. Some people find it sinister, full of echoes of war, and others say that it looks like a flight of insects – bees or dragonflies. It could have been shot from an accompanying helicopter, although the sharpness of the image would seem to suggest that it would have required a very high shutter speed, probably out of keeping with the available light, so it is more likely that the photographer was on the ground.

133. *Photographer:* Edmund Nägele
   Camera: Pentax 6×7
   Lens: 150mm
   Exposure: 1/60 at f8
   Film: Ektachrome

Shooting landscapes above Ross Creek, in Montana, the photographer noticed this helicopter, probably patrolling for the forestry service, on the lookout for fires, and he waited until the aircraft was contrasted against a dark, shadowed part of the forest before making his shot. Normally seen as quite a large machine, the helicopter looks tiny in this natural setting.

134. *Photographer:* Edmund Nägele
   Camera: Pentax 6×7
   Lens: 1,000mm
   Exposure: 1/30 at f16
   Film: Ektachrome

Not, as might perhaps be supposed, the meanderings of a drunken road marker! The photographer took this picture for its curiosity and amusement value in Eldorado Hills, California, and it shows the road markings as Eldorado County Road ends at the Sacramento County Line.

135. *Photographer:* Edmund Nägele
   Camera: Pentax 6×7
   Lens: 1,000mm
   Exposure: 1/60 at f8
   Film: Ektachrome

San Francisco's California Street, with its cable-cars that seem, indeed, to 'reach halfway to the stars', appears to progress like a giant staircase and this effect has been accentuated by the use of a very long lens which has compressed the apparent distances so that cars in the distance appear almost the same size as those in the foreground and the lines of the receding tracks of the tramway show very little convergence. This is an effect typical of long lenses, but it is much more apparent in a subject such as this. The photographer waited for periods of up to thirty minutes between shots in order to get, each time, a cable-car outlined at the top of the hill, as well as people, to complete his composition.

136. *Photographer:* Edmund Nägele
   Camera: Pentax 6×7
   Lens: 105mm
   Exposure: 1/15 at f16
   Film: Ektachrome

Edmund Nägele invariably carries with him, when he goes on assignments, several rolls of film on which he has already exposed subjects such as moons, suns etc., in different positions in the frame, and in different sizes. They are all, of course, kept with notes as to what is on each frame and where. Apart from keeping exact records, this is not too difficult to do on 35mm film, and is very simple on sheet film, but on 120 roll film there is the problem of re-rolling the film in its backing paper and re-running it through the camera in such a way as to ensure that the previously-exposed subjects fall in exactly the area required on the second exposure. Sometimes, as in this shot of Delicate Arch in Arches National Park, Utah, the object is not natural at all. This effect was created by cutting a hole out of a piece of black card and positioning a torch behind it, shining through a yellow gel and with a cross star filter on the lens; all accomplished in a mobile camper, at night!

137. *Photographer:* Edmund Nägele
   Camera: Pentax 6×7
   Lens: 105mm plus extension tube
   Exposure: 1/30 at f16
   Film: Ektachrome

Rocky Mountain poppies at Lake Louise, Alberta, Canada. The yellow poppy heads and seed cases stand out well against the blue sky and the clouds. If you are lucky enough to find flowers growing at the top of high ground – a small hillock, perhaps – then there is less difficulty in getting rid of the background and shooting against the sky in order to isolate and accentuate their delicate structure. Usually, however, things are not as easy as that and it is a matter of mounting the camera on a tripod that has provision for very low mounting; using a ground spike fitted with a ball and socket head, or using some other object such as a camera bag on which to rest the camera near to ground level. It is here that a removable finder, allowing you to look down into the finder well rather than having to lie full-length behind the camera trying to squint up at the subject, comes in most useful.

138. *Photographer:* Edmund Nägele
   Camera: Pentax 6×7
   Lens: 150mm
   Exposure: See following details
   Film: Ektachrome

In this shot of a thunderstorm passing over Halkett Lake, Saskatchewan, in Canada, or, indeed, in any electrical storm, it would be highly unlikely that all the flashes would take place at the same time. The only really successful way to catch the drama of such an occasion is, when the storm is approaching, to set the camera on a tripod, choose an aperture of, say, f11, and to open the shutter on 'time' or hold it down on 'B' with the aid of a locking cable release, and wait for the flashes to occur as the storm passes across the frame. Obviously, luck plays an important part, as well as anticipation, in taking such pictures and in this particular subject the impact has been dramatically increased because there was a stretch of water between the photographer and the storm in which the reflections of the lightning flashes have been caught.

139. *Photographer:* Edmund Nägele
   Camera: Pentax 6×7
   Lens: 55mm
   Exposure: Not recorded
   Film: Ektachrome

A beautiful, geometrically composed photograph of the Muttart Conservatory in Edmonton, Alberta, Canada. The conservatory provides a controlled-environment growing area unique in North America. Each of the pyramids contains the flora of a specific climatic zone. The ornamental lake in the foreground reflects the shapes of the pyramids and the contrasting geometric patterns of the buildings in the background, and the photographer used a graduated filter to dramatize the color of the sky.

140. *Photographer:* Peter Pugh-Cook
Camera: Hasselblad
Lens: 80mm
Exposure: 1/30 at f8
Film: Ektachrome

Soft daylight through the window was the only illumination for this mother and baby subject. The shot is, therefore, primarily backlit except for some light reflected by the light-colored walls of the room. The mother and child have been arranged in exactly the right position to take advantage of the attractive shape of the window with its leaded panes, and the nightdress has been deliberately rumpled and creased to add to the authentic feeling of the shot and to get away from the impression that it could be an advertisement for nightwear.

141. *Photographer:* David Gibbon
Camera: Nikon FE
Lens: 43-86 zoom at 86mm setting
Exposure: On automatic – not recorded
Film: Kodachrome 64

To a small child the sea is very big. You have to summon up courage to venture into it. It helps to have someone older with you; someone who understands these things and will hold your hand. This was the scene that the photographer saw being enacted in front of him on a soft, summer evening on the south coast of England. He grabbed a camera and took the shot quickly, managing to capture, in the position of the figures, the older girl's reassuring attitude and the younger child's trepidation.

142. *Photographer:* Douglass Baglin
Camera: 5 × 4 fitted with 6 × 9 rollfilm back
Lens: Not recorded
Exposure: Not recorded
Film: Ektachrome

The technique used for photographing large firework displays, such as this one in Australia, is much the same as that used for recording lightning flashes. The first thing to do is to determine the exact area in which the display will take place and then set up the camera on a tripod to frame this area. A small aperture can be used, particularly if there are quite brightly lit buildings in the frame, and then at the appropriate moment the shutter can be opened on 'time' or locked open on 'B' with the aid of a locking cable release. A number of photographers prefer to open the shutter and then cover it with a piece of dark card, uncovering the lens as the fireworks form their patterns. How long the exposure should take will depend on the intensity of the fireworks and how many different effects you wish to record on one exposure. One starburst or whatever will not usually have much impact, but too many will tend to burn out the area in which they are exploding and the individual trails will be lost.

143. *Photographer:* Edmund Nägele
Camera: Pentax 6 × 7
Lens: 105mm
Exposure: 1/250 at f8
Film: Ektachrome

The expanse of dark water, with the cargo ship and three sailing boats seeming like toys on its surface, was photographed from an aircraft flying above English Bay, Vancouver, in British Columbia, Canada. The photographer had hired the 'plane in order to take aerial shots of the

Vancouver area but he saw this subject and thought it made an interesting composition. He used a fairly high shutter speed, not so much to counteract movement but rather to try to offset the effects of vibration, which is always a problem when shooting from aircraft. He also used an ultra-violet absorption filter to cut through haze. Because he was content to let the sea appear dark, rather than showing any detail in it, he based his exposure on the ships.

144. *Photographer:* Photri
Camera: Nikon F
Lens: Not recorded
Exposure: Not recorded
Film: Ektachrome

This is a fairly straightforward picture of a Solar eclipse. The moon has already partly obscured the sun's disc. Such photographs are not difficult to take, but they do demand a substantial tripod on which to mount the camera fitted with a long lens. For really dramatic close-ups the camera would need to be mounted, via an adaptor, to a telescope. The exposure would probably have been in the region of 1/60 at f5.6-f8 and at this sort of shutter speed an item such as an equatorial drive would not be necessary.

145. *Photographer:* Edmund Nägele
Camera: Pentax 6 × 7
Lens: 55mm
Exposure: 1/30 at f22
Film: Agfachrome 50 S

This huge cactus, photographed at the Organ Pipe Cactus National Monument in Arizona, has been made to look even larger by silhouetting it, together with the trees, against the evening sky. As a wide-angle lens was used, stopped down to allow considerable depth of field, and we have no indication within the picture as to how far behind the cactus the trees actually were, we could imagine that the cactus towered high above them, and only our knowledge of the actual sizes that they grow to can tell us that this is not the case. The photographer made the shot using a film on which he had previously exposed the sun, using a long lens, as he felt that this would add something to the unreality of the scene.

146. *Photographer:* Edmund Nägele
Camera: Pentax 6 × 7
Lens: 55mm
Exposure: 1/60 at f16
Film: Ektachrome

Snow, having very high reflecting properties, can lead the photographer into serious error in estimating exposure. If a straight reading is taken and used, it will result in underexposure and the snow will have a distinct blue cast. The normal procedure is to take this into account and to increase exposure by 1½-2 stops over that indicated. For this picture, Edmund Nägele decided, however, not to do this but to use the underexposure and blueness to suggest moonlight, and he therefore took his picture using a film that he had previously exposed on shots of the moon taken, in fact, in England some weeks previously.

147. *Photographer:* Neil Sutherland
Camera: Hasselblad
Lens: 80mm
Exposure: 1/30 at f8
Film: Ektachrome Professional

While photographing a firework display on Guy Fawkes' night in Ripley, Surrey, Neil Sutherland saw the patterns that were being made by the flames of the bonfire as they danced in the air. He took a reading straight from the fire itself and made his exposure, using a shutter speed slow enough to record the movement in the flames but one that he felt confident of hand-holding.

148. *Photographer:* Michel Folco
     Camera: Nikkormat EL
     Lens: 105mm
     Exposure: On automatic – not recorded
     Film: Kodachrome 25

The desert areas near the Pyramids in Egypt are well-trodden by tourists, camels and local people catering for visitors' needs. Towards the end of a day's shooting, when most of the people had departed, the photographer saw this lone Arab striding purposefully to his destination. He was attracted by the solitary figure in the middle of the empty space, and made his exposure with his camera set on automatic.

149. *Photographer:* K. Ojutkangas
     No technical details available

A classic sunset seen across the waters of a lake in Finland. The exposure has been judged exactly, so that the setting sun's rays stand out well against the water, but there is still plenty of detail in the landscape.

150. *Photographer:* Neil Sutherland
     Camera: Arca-Swiss 5×4
     Lens: 90mm Super Angulon
     Exposure: 1/30 at f11
     Film: Agfachrome 50 S

Selsey Lifeboat Station, Sussex, in January. A nicely-balanced composition, backlit by a hazy sun, which has allowed the photographer to concentrate on the lifeboat station and its bridge by throwing them into silhouette, while at the same time there is enough light to pick up details in the sea and the beach. The breakwater in the foreground is in just the right position to hold the composition and bring it back into the picture area.

151. *Photographer:* Robert Matassa
     Camera: 5×4 View
     Lens: 180mm
     Exposure: 1/30 at f22
     Film: Ektachrome

A frosty morning at Loch Garry, in Scotland, provided the setting for this picture of the delicate tracery of trees forming filigree patterns against the sun. The backlighting has also enhanced the shapes in the frost-covered foreground. When we first start taking photographs we are taught that the light source should always be behind us, and this, of course, is true for a number of subjects. It is surprising, however, to see how many successful pictures break this rule – always providing the photographer knows exactly what he is doing and how to achieve the effect he wants.

152. *Photographer:* Neil Sutherland
     Camera: Arca-Swiss 5×4
     Lens: 90mm Super Angulon
     Exposure: 1 minute at f16
     Film: Agfachrome 50 S

It might reasonably be supposed that if, for instance, an exposure of 1 second at f4 was considered 'correct' for a given subject, then, according to the laws of reciprocity, 32 seconds at f22 would give the same result. Unfortunately, however, this is not so. Films do behave according to this law within the range of about 1/1000 of a second and 1 second, depending on the film used, and this is adequate for most photographic purposes, but this law breaks down when very short or very long exposures are required and this breakdown is known as reciprocity law failure. At exposures outside this range, night shots for instance when considerably longer exposures than 1 second may be called for, the emulsion speed of the film becomes effectively and progressively slower. This is something that must always be taken into account when deciding on exposure. Different manufacturers' emulsions vary as to the factor that should be applied and the use of color-correcting filters in such instances and this information is normally either packed with the film or is available from the manufacturer on request.

Big Ben's Clock Tower, the Houses of Parliament and Parliament Square, London. As may be seen from the clock face, the photograph was made at six o'clock in the evening and the time of the year was March. In temperate climates this is very often the ideal time of the year for night photography. In the summer there is often a haze present which can affect sharpness, particularly in the distance, but the biggest drawback to summer shooting is having to wait until very late in the evening before the sun really goes down and street lighting, or floodlighting takes over as the main light source. Even in the early part of the year there is enough light in the sky for it to register as blue, as in this shot. The photographer obtained permission to go onto the roof of the Treasury building to make his exposure and, judging from the number of times the picture has been used, his efforts were well worth while.

153. *Photographer:* Per Eide
     Camera: Mamiya RB67
     Lens: 50mm
     Exposure: Not recorded
     Film: Agfachrome 50 S

London's famous Oxford Street at Christmas time. The photographer chose a high viewpoint to show the street stretching into the distance and he kept his exposure as short as he could – a few seconds – because he wanted to use the red, London buses as foreground interest but he wanted as little movement as possible in them. At this point in Oxford Street there are a number of bus stops and traffic lights, so there is always a reasonable chance of finding at least some buses stationary.

154. *Photographer:* Edmund Nägele
     Camera: Pentax 6×7
     Lens: 150mm
     Exposure: 1/2 second at f8
     Film: High Speed Ektachrome rated 640 ASA

San Francisco's Chinatown – about as Chinese as anything can possibly look outside Hong Kong – was the subject for this night shot. Because of the number of vehicles and pedestrians moving throughout the lower part of the picture, Edmund Nägele decided to up-rate his film by two stops – and, obviously, marked his film for extended development – so that he could use a fast enough shutter speed to show only minimal movement.

155. *Photographer:* Chris Harvey
     Camera: Hasselblad
     Lens: 150mm
     Exposure: 1/125 at f5.6
     Film: Ektachrome

This appealing and apparently simple picture is not, perhaps, quite as simple as it appears. We know that it pleases, but if it is considered carefully it soon becomes apparent that everything about it is just right and carefully planned: the position of the girl in the ferns, the choice of a fairly open aperture to throw all but the girl and the area in which she stands into soft focus, the soft colors of her clothes, and her position against the area of heavy shadow. making sure that, when backlit, all the viewer's attention would be directed towards her face and hair, and the basket of colorful flowers she is holding.

156. *Photographer:* Roy Day
   Camera: MPP Mark VII 5×4
   Lens: 150mm Symmar
   Exposure: 1 second at f32
   Film: Agfachrome 50 S

Shot for an American publisher, this is a typical low-key picture taken in the studio with the aid of tungsten lights. The greatest problem with this particular shot was obtaining authentic fruits, vegetables and leaves. The arrangement was pretty much left to the photographer, except that the client required a dark area left at the top of the picture for lettering.

157. *Photographer:* Photri
   Camera: Nikon F
   Lens: Not recorded
   Exposure: Not recorded
   Film: Agfachrome 50 S

A picture to alarm the ecologists! This shot was taken at the Westvaco Plant, Covington, Texas, and the somber, rain-laden sky adds to the heavy feeling of 'Satanic Mills'. There is little to comment on regarding the photograph itself; the picture was seen by the photographer and, despite the poor weather, he realized that there was a shot to be made.

158. *Photographer:* Beverley Goodway
   Camera: Mamiya RB67
   Lens: 127mm
   Exposure: 1/60 at f8
   Film: Ektachrome

A charming study of a little girl by the sea. All the attention is focused on the child, leaving the sea to go unsharp; the moment has been chosen to make the exposure just as the foam swirled around her ankles, and the hat, bucket and spade – and their colors – are nicely-chosen touches that finish off the composition.

159. *Photographer:* Edmund Nägele
   Camera: Pentax 6×7
   Lens: 55mm
   Exposure: 1/60 at f11
   Film: Ektachrome

Kepuhi Bay Beach, Molokai, Hawaii, was the setting for this picture. The photographer was primarily interested in the changing textures of the foreground rocks, the drier sand, the wet sand and the sea – all accentuated by backlighting. He used a wide-angle lens stopped well down to give good depth of field, although this was governed by the necessity to use a reasonably fast shutter speed to hold movement in the waves at the water's edge. The figure of the girl was placed near the reflection of the sun in the water to balance the composition, pulling the eye away from the foreground shapes.

160. *Photographer:* Will Curwen
   Camera: Pentax 6×7
   Lens: 150mm

Exposure: 1/30 at f11
   Film: Agfachrome 50 S

Sunset at Pond Village Beach, North Truro, Cape Cod, Massachusetts. A calm, golden sea – almost lake-like in its tranquility – and an equally peaceful sky attracted the photographer and he made his exposure including, as a contrast, the man made structure, though exactly what it is, or what purpose it serves, the photographer didn't say.

161. *Photographer:* Mike Hughes
   No technical details available
   Film: Agfachrome 50 S

It may be argued that sunsets have become rather hackneyed as subject matter, but there is something about them that makes it hard to resist taking the camera out and making an exposure. Sunset over water has a particular appeal and if there are boats present as well – then so much the better. This sunset subject, with the fishing boats almost in silhouette against the evening sky, was photographed at Leigh on Sea, in Essex.

162. *Photographer:* Robert Matassa
   Camera: Mamiya RB67
   Lens: 127mm
   Exposure: 1/60 at f16
   Film: Ektachrome

Sanur Beach lies on the East coast of Bali, in Indonesia. During a recent trip to the island the photographer took to rising at six o'clock every morning, long before any tourists were around, to take advantage of something they were missing – and which, he adds, he felt was very much their loss – namely the delicately beautiful sunrises and the particular quality of light that is to be found each morning; quite different from the West coast of the island, where the sun may be seen to set, but which is an altogether more garish affair. This shot of the sunrise was one of the results of his early morning forays.

163. *Photographer:* Douglass Baglin
   Camera: Hasselblad
   Lens: 80mm
   Exposure: 1/60 at f16
   Film: Ektachrome

This shot of a hot-air balloon, filled and ready to cast off, was taken at Hunter's Hill, New South Wales, Australia.

164. *Photographer:* Jim Kingshott
   Camera: Mamiya C3
   Lens: 180mm
   Exposure: 1/500 at f16
   Film: Agfachrome 50 S

Having spent the day shooting landscapes, country cottages and the like, Jim Kingshott was passing Heathrow Airport, near London when he saw in the distance the unmistakable shape of Concorde as it came in to land. He barely had time to grab his camera, set the exposure, focus and shoot before the aircraft was out of frame. When shooting aircraft, Jim regularly tries to include the sun and underexposes by four stops to create a 'moonlight' effect and it is a technique that works very well, providing the subject, which is invariably rendered in silhouette, has a distinct and recognizable shape.

165. *Photographer:* Ian McDonald
   Camera: Nikon F2
   Lens: 28mm
   Exposure: 1/125 at f11
   Film: Kodachrome 64